SUCCESS MANTRAS AND MUSINGS

EDUPRENEUR MANJULA POOJA SHROFF

Anurita Rathore Jadeja

Vitasta
LET KNOWLEDGE SPREAD

Published by
Renu Kaul Verma
Vitasta Publishing Pvt Ltd
2/15, Ansari Road, Daryaganj
New Delhi-110 002
info@vitastapublishing.com

ISBN 978-93-90961-14-6

First Edition 2022
Second Reprint 2022

MRP ₹ 595

Edited by Kanagam King
Layout and Cover by Somesh Kumar Mishra
Printed by Chaman Enterprises, Delhi

To the cheerful unbeatable spirit
of Manjula Pooja Shroff.
And Sanyukta Kumari Rathore
for filling me with joie de vivre
and deep love.

CONTENTS

PREFACE

Success Mantras and Musings – Edupreneur Manjula Pooja Shroff is the story of a journey, a story of dreams accomplished, challenges overcome, and faith heightened.

The book gives an insight into the thoughts and learnings of entrepreneur-educator Manjula Pooja Shroff, who, by virtue of running educational institutions and social work, has gained tremendous understanding of human behaviour and management, besides grasping well the art of turning possibilities into reality.

From leading an exclusive life at Surangi Palace, Ichapuram in Odisha, in her formative years and then moving into a hostel yet taking charge of managing home, staff and finance, to dealing with the loss of her closest ones at a young age and then moving into a world far beyond home, Manjula hasn't gone by any rulebook to achieve success but has firmly followed her gut and stayed focussed. Self-belief, besides learning from experience and people around her, has ensured that the vision is clear and the efforts are constant.

I have penned this book in the voice of Manjula to establish a direct connect with readers and also create a link where thoughts are shared, beliefs expressed and experiences highlighted from an eventful, meaningful and progressive life. The sensitivity and strength, dedication and determination of the subject are a major pull for not just me as a writer but anyone who knows even remotely about the ebullient Manjula and her raison d'etre.

Early chapters of the book focus on her childhood days, her immediate folks, taking on responsibilities, her early rebellion and the beginning of her entrepreneurial journey. Coming to Indian Institute of Management, Ahmedabad changed the course of her personal and professional life.

Few chapters focus on her understanding of relationships, early projects and how she started and established schools and institutions under Kalorex Foundation. While the subject of women empowerment holds significance, the chapter on motherhood and the bond between the mother and the child are heart-warming and relatable. Chapters on travel and outdoor interests give a sneak-peak not only into her life but also take readers on a fun-filled journey with generous life lessons sprinkled on.

The book has nineteen chapters that outline and delve into her life learnings. Various subheads have been provided for quick reference and easy reading, depending on the reader's area of immediate interest. This enables them to pick randomly for reading without having to bother about the sequence of the chapters.

The chapters don't just cover the different facets of Manjula's life, they offer rich experiences, ideas, and examples of living that drive to excel, nurture young minds, support individual journeys and, above all, encourage faith and self-reliance.

Anurita Rathore Jadeja

FOREWORD

'Change the world by being yourself' may be Amy Poehler's line but Manjula Pooja Shroff has lived it and Anurita Rathore Jadeja has loved it enough to write this book.

Celebrating a life lived in earnest pursuit and die-hard dreams with tireless efforts is validation most noble. Being a woman in a man's world is tough and to be a successful woman in business enterprise, a haloed domain of man, is tougher! The author and her muse, therefore, deserve much acclaim.

Providence chooses our place and birth, our parents and the potential encrypted in our genes, but each individual life's journey is unique as per his or her choice of path, drive, compulsions and commitments. And these account for the sum total of experiences gathered and achievements garnered. For anybody to bring out in words the subtle sensitive kaleidoscope of intellectual, emotional, spiritual energy that erupts, sparkles, explodes and flows mesmerizingly in each experience of agony, in lengthy periods of struggles, and ecstasy of earned moments of achievements and glory, during the life journey of a person is a huge challenge; Anurita has excelled herself and marvellously at that.

The life experiences of Manjula that have transformed her to the personality she is today is unmistakably mirrored as vibrantly in the pages as her vivacious self. The reader will be gently cajoled to partake of the flow of tide of times which may sometimes seem familiar, sometimes evoke surprise and admiration, or may even go on to inspire.

Having a connect with Anurita, and a deeper connect with Manjula as family, bestows on me the happy privilege to acknowledge with gratitude to Anurita for this seamless sharing of a life dedicated to excellence.

The human birth is the pinnacle, the summum bonum of existence on earth. Any human being who learns, understands and strives to be deserves to be celebrated, and one who shares the knowledge with others, more so!

Manoja Manjari Devi

Manjula Pooja Shroff

→

Every life is a story, slightly more interesting than can be imagined. The gift of experience is what turns it into a masterpiece.

CHAPTER ONE

Tabula Rasa

It must be the early months, the initial days of existence and survival, that go on to shape your life. Perhaps everything, good and bad, hardships and glory, flow through as though planned to precision. And yet, you realise, time and again, that you have the steering wheel in your hands. Is life a result of our choices or are we led to what we are meant to achieve? Perhaps a good blend is far more likely.

Unwanted but Revered

Occasionally, I like to take a trip down memory lane. I like to reminisce about my childhood which was filled with love – my mother's love.

There was nothing I feared, nobody that made me feel I wasn't the centre of her existence. But how my life began is rather different. I was unwanted, well almost. I have, from the womb, been a fighter. My mother, Rani Soubhagya Manjari

Devi was only seventeen when she had her first child, my sister, Manoja Manjari Devi. My infant sister was taken away by Rani Srimati Devi, my maternal grandmother, Srimati Laxman Manjari's elder sister. She had also adopted my mother and raised her. We affectionately addressed her as Didi. My sister was barely four months old when I was conceived; thus driving away any notions that I was a desirable, looked-forward-to child.

Even after I was born, my father, Raja Keerti Chandra Deo did not see me for twenty-one days. The reasons were superstitious, but given by the scholarly who understood and read birth charts, and hence had to be followed.

Bachcha dikhana nahi tha is what I learnt from others. There was another twist soon after. My father's industrialist friend wanted to adopt me but my mother, uncharacteristically so, did not want to let me go. In most matters, she didn't quite have a say.

In my growing up years, I never saw my mother ever fight for her rights; she was reticent and quiet, emotionally very vulnerable. This made me extremely protective of her even at a very tender age. I became her confidante. She never stopped me from doing anything.

It was a relationship based on immense love for each other. She supported me in everything I did or wanted to do, which I realised, was a major boost for my confidence. She either had decided opinions or none at all, but all that I saw and grew up knowing was that I was the apple of her eye. After a few years, my brother was born, later addressed as Raja Hrudaya Chandra Deo, my younger and more adventurous comrade. But I still remained my mother's favourite.

When 'The End' Came Too Soon

Death is eventual and embraces all, but in my life it changed a lot of things, and has been a turning point. My father's younger brother, Jay Chandra Deo was the most significant male influence in my life but when I was all of fifteen, he passed away due to cancer.

He was unmarried and somehow that directed all his attention and affection towards the children of the family, I enjoying the larger share. His death was a tremendous blow. A couple of years after his death, Didi passed away. They were both my strong anchors and their death hastened my growth.

My teenage years were spent feeling helpless for not being old enough to manage everything, be in charge of and tend to situations that seemed out of control and emotionally devastating. How often I wished I wasn't so young!

Another incident that is etched in memory is when my mother was really unwell. I must have been not more than ten. The doctor, while suggesting something, asked, *Koi bada nahin hai kya*? (Is there no elder around?) I still remember desperately wishing I was older, but nonetheless, along the way I realized I was still capable.

By the time I was twenty years old, I was an invincible person, with no distractions, no teen hangover, no relationships; nothing that was usual in the life of a young girl existed in my radar. However, the worst was yet to come – a time no child wishes to encounter, a day you wish you could delete from your life. My mother, my core, left the world and all I recollect is feeling numb, lifeless and beaten. The road ahead was blurred and yet one had to keep going. Along the way, life simply forced me to grow up.

Life in the Golden Cage

What it is to live in abundance is something I have always known. Right from childhood, I have had it all – love, privileges, and everything favourable. I could ask for anything, it was at my beck and call. Good life was around for the asking and 'no' was a word that did not exist for me.

School life was loads of excitement, and being popular only added to it. But dancing and singing was taboo, so was wearing jeans and frocks. Even when I went to the theatre, someone would accompany me. It was a caged feeling, and ironical how despite all privileges, there was always a huge list of things I couldn't do. In fact, certain chores only the maids could do. But there was an abundance of love, care and affection. The extent to which people accommodated me might seem unreal too. But I felt it was my right, be it the people around or the things I had. How could I not be loved, is how I grew up thinking and feeling! In hindsight, you realise, things come to you in excess and then they are equalled in other ways. Some things come too soon, and are snatched away equally quick. Life, I believe, teaches you lessons for the future. Looking back, I have no regrets. No matter what, I am a fighter. I fight and I learn and am honest to a fault. Reviewing situations does make you wonder if things could have been handled differently, but my faith in self and God has been tremendous. That is perhaps what has helped me survive ordeals that could have perhaps sunk another.

Early Departure from Home

What does any normal five-year-old do? Play around, ask for goodies when hungry and periodically run to parents for warm, reassuring hugs. As for me, I was sent off to St Joseph's Convent in Cuttack at that age. I would visit home twice a year. Those would be times of indulgence, when uttering a word meant wishes being granted. Getting pampered was the order of the day.

I would take a call on various matters as well, and along the way, learn something new. For instance, yoga. No one taught me yoga; it is something I learnt from a magazine. It is almost as if my body had an intelligence of its own. I realised yoga is a way to access intelligence, it is faith, it is resolve. I learnt and accessed something new each time I came home and felt like a boss.

Despite staying at a hostel for the major part of the year, I was a home bird. It was only in Surangi Palace, our ancestral house, that I felt at home, I felt I belonged.

In fact, I must have been only in grade five when I started making decisions and being involved in all matters relating to the household. What fuelled my confidence was that my mother would let me do it... whatever be it, nothing was ever contested.

I grew up way earlier than other children, and taking up responsibility came naturally to me. Besides, toeing customs, not for the sake of it, but because I believed in something, was very crucial to me. Like, sitting at home for puja is something I believed in, nobody had to force me to be there.

All said and done, wherever I'd be, at home or hostel, there were silent moments when everything around seemed to pause, and a feeling of being looked-after enveloped me. It was this way while I was a little girl, it continued when I left Odisha and went to Delhi, and has remained with me up till today.

Education, the Greatest Binder

I confronted death in the most crucial years of my life. During that period, I lost the ones I was closest to. This changed the course of my life. That is when I turned inwards. Something within told me that though they were gone physically, they were still connected to me. Thus, amid thoughts that consoled and confused, I arrived at a crucial point where education became my primary refuge. Education was going to be not just necessary but very integral to everything else that would follow in my journey. I knew only with a good education, I could shape my life and become someone worthy of emulation, someone who could lead for others to relate to and follow. Very early in life I learnt that education is your core vehicle, your means to an end.

It is only passing years that gave me answers to the doubts I harboured and led my plans to suitable and deserving conclusions.

Graduating Joys

After a memorable school and hostel life in St Joseph's Convent in Cuttack, I pursued graduation at Ramadevi Women's College in Bhubaneswar. I stayed with my sister and attended college regularly. Three years later, I joined Utkal University for a post-graduation program in Political Science as well. Little did I know that soon my life would take me away from Odisha.

The education and the process, back in the days, was a fine blend of life lessons and knowledge empowerment. I think I grew up inordinately quick owing to all that was happening around me.

My sense of responsibility stopped me from being myself on multiple occasions; I had tremendous foresight and could see how taking things frivolously could detract me from creating a meaningful future. What I didn't know, however, was that the near future would bring to me my biggest setback. And that too, sooner rather than later. The event of my mother passing away while I was still on the better side of my twenties is what led to my decision to move to Delhi.

I took up a programme in soft skills learning, a computer course at NIIT, and also a part-time job at the Centre for Professional Development in Higher Education. Life took a drastic turn. Now I was staying in a little terrace room, better known as *barsaati*, travelling in DTC buses, learning to cook, wash and stand in queues. But the picture wasn't grim; it was a new life, an escape from where I had come from. I eventually broke free from everything. In my mid-twenties, months after the last surviving elder of the family, my father, passed away, I arrived at Indian Institute of Management in Ahmedabad. It was the summer of 1993 when I first met Pratul on campus. Months later, he proposed marriage, and today, years later, Ahmedabad is home.

How far have I actually come? What guided me here? Did I make it happen? These questions have enjoyed a round of hide and seek with me for at least three decades, periodically nudging me, if not pursuing me stridently. The only answer I can still seemingly find is that whatever has been, was meant to be.

If the purpose of life is to figure out the riddle of death, I have had the

advantage of an early training, way before my teenage years.

I got to play the elder sister, despite being the younger one. Born into a royal household, but running it even before I was ten, fate had an interesting way of gifting me with experiences.

CHAPTER TWO

First In Line, Born To Lead

I was the middle child in a royal household, but gears changed as life had other plans in store. An elder sister and a younger brother, having siblings meant always having company, be it turning for support or playing guide. Over the years, I have often seen single children rueing for a sibling, wishing they had someone to share their fun times with, to enjoy games and adventures with, to play pranks and stick together if ever singled out.

On the other hand, I have also seen siblings fight, be intolerant of each other or have very different interests and hobbies, enough to prefer journeying solo. Being witness to all kinds – single child, twins, more than two siblings, as well as kids brought up in a joint family – you realise there is no specific classification or mandate that works when it comes to deciding what is ideal. There are no specific examples to confirm if children with siblings are happier than those without. Their confidence levels and learning abilities don't necessarily reflect this aspect either.

Born into royalty can also fetch you a diverse set of experiences, some a result of notions you possibly find tough to brush aside, others owing to knowledge and lifestyle inherited over generations. There are some who treat you with reverence and some who look up to you in awe. But growing up in a family that respects age-old traditions can throw up challenges while also settle the dust.

Sister Shelter

In my case, though I was born second, life changed after my elder sister got adopted. I was very young. I neither understood what was happening nor do I recall any strong emotions felt back then. She and I went to the same boarding school, so to me she was always my elder sister, looking after me. I was the naughty, carefree one, and she was always protective. All through the year, we were together; it was only during vacations that she went to a different home. That is perhaps the only time I missed having someone to turn to, for advice or for support.

I played the role of a follower and leader equally well; my sister would guide me in academics. She would correct me when wrong, teach me the dos and don'ts, how to be more serious and focussed in academics rather than in co-curricular activities. On the other hand, I was also an elder sister. I remember taking care of my brother, trying to feed him, singing lullabies to make him sleep.

There surely is something special about being the eldest child. Generally, firstborns are expected to be more caring, responsible and protective of their younger siblings. Not only have I realised this in our case, I have seen many elder children being kindly disposed towards their younger sisters and brothers. As per theory, the oldest is more authoritarian, perhaps owing to expectations of parents and the special welcome they receive. The youngest child is often the spoilt baby of the household who, in most cases, is especially favoured by the parents. It is normally the middle child who is even-tempered but has trouble fitting in, being sandwiched between the younger and the older sibling. Since I was both, the middle child and in many ways the older child, I have varied traits.

Middle-Child Syndrome

Looking back at my growing up years, I remember having the constant need to prove myself. I suspect this to be a middle-child syndrome; since they think they don't have a firm footing at home, they are inclined to subconsciously prove themselves. Many also believe that children of this order get ignored, remain unnoticed or even outright neglected. I am not sure how true this stands for me but I recall Alfred Adler's middle-child syndrome theory which says that although children may be born into the same household, their birth order greatly influences their psychological development. If the theory is to be believed, the middle children have to fend for themselves and even rough it out. In hindsight, this stood me in good ground since life can pretty much throw anything at you and you might need to bend, duck or fend for yourself.

I have had my fair share of struggles while finding my place in the family. Circumstances and situations so unfolded that I began taking mature decisions at an early age which eventually shaped me into the person I am now. Even today, I may be a strong-minded person, but I still work for my place under the sun, I still go through jitters while launching a new project, and have butterflies in the stomach when I stand on stage and speak to thousands of people. My early years of fighting to ride a bicycle, later taught me how very like cycling life is – maintaining a balance even while moving forward.

Being an 'Adult' Child

Of all the things I may have been, I clearly recall being responsible and responsive, both as a child and early teenager. Ready to take initiatives, I was always eager to try new things. Being energetic came naturally to me and what I now feel proud of is having immense clarity of thought even back then. Decision-making is a very empowering trait. The more decisions one takes, the better one gets. Being heard and taken seriously in most situations was a huge confidence booster. It was like an anchorage, a support which I felt I received all the more when I turned elder sister to my younger sibling. It is perhaps then that seeds of leadership were sown. Also, with my father being away most of the time and my mother being ill, I had little choice but to behave responsibly. In the household, I was thrown into situations that needed an adult to attend to and that is how I began to essay that leadership role early on in life. However, none of the importance bestowed on me saw me getting carried away. That was only because I inherently knew I was always much loved. I was my mother's pet and thus needed no further validation to feel important.

Over time, as I grew up in the palace, I began to behave more like an adult. Understanding what was expected of me was easier and hence, there was lesser questioning and more acceptance of my actions and decisions. With time, I also figured there were social norms unique to royal families that had been passed on from ancient times. There were times I felt some rules and traditions needed revision to fit in the contemporary mould. Though, that clearly wasn't the thought adhered to by many others. Traditions and culture systems were celebrated with aplomb, so what if they were ancient, medieval or even slightly uncomfortable. Live and let live – it was very early in life that I learnt to appreciate this, perhaps even before I turned ten! So from a very young age I began to shoulder responsibility. Leadership, therefore, is second nature and I find it easy to reach out to people at large, understand them and their issues. But on the other hand, being from a royal household, one is also taught to maintain a certain reserve and aloofness which is often mistaken for arrogance by people.

Of Royal Charms

There is a sense of reverence and awe for royal families in society. People are intrigued by their lifestyle, their traditions, norms and customs. I often wondered if it was karma, since it is a privilege and thus considered good karma to be born into a royal household. I experienced it while growing up. Whether at school or in social gatherings, I got recognised because of my royal lineage back in Odisha. It was particularly awkward when much older people touched our feet or even prostrated before us. My friends teasingly called me *jema* since princesses are thus addressed in Odisha.

A Life of Restrictions

No one knows better the life than the ones who are born into it.

Restrictions were a natural aspect of my upbringing. Growing up in our palatial home, I had the tendency to question anything and everything that did not seem all right, normal or easy, but I never challenged anything or anyone.

I would grumble for a bit but eventually follow the rules that were laid down. Being a girl, there were more restrictions, restrictions relating to what we could wear, places we could go to, how and whom we could speak to, besides general social demeanour.

In quieter moments, I often wished there weren't so many dos and don'ts for women. Men had far fewer restrictions. I wasn't allowed to wear trousers or ride a bike. I wasn't allowed to act on stage if there were boys too; short hair was a strict no, and socialising with all and sundry wasn't taken kindly to. It is only many years later, when I went to college, that a lot of things changed for me.

I could think for myself and decide on smaller aspects involving day-to-day comforts, including the clothes I wore or the length of hair I kept. And then, there came a time when no one could dictate to me anymore.

Early Empowerment Lessons

Almost everything you really learn is from all that you see around you. Whether you choose to stay in line with the positive norms or ignore them to pursue a rough course has a lot to do with your mental accommodation of the situation as well as understanding of right and wrong.

My family had always been very philanthropic. Be they schools, colleges, hospitals, temples, community centres, sports areas, public drinking water stations, sanitation systems, all were either built or donated for by my forefathers. Being a chip off that block, I always identified with giving and doing good for others. I knew no other way and figured very early the joys of giving. I understood how empowering the joy and act of contributing to a life or a community or society is. Somewhere as I grew up, I also realised that giving is a mind-set and is not proportionate to the material wealth one possesses. You can own a lot but be dismissive of helping those in need, or ironically, you could have very little but want to share it with others. The gesture of giving, thankfully as I realised, is in your mind.

As a little girl who ran around the entire palace, observing things and sometimes reacting too, I realised, and uneasily so, that strangely the customs and laws were enforced by the managers at the palace and the women caretakers who had been there for generations. I found that being caretakers and house managers for as long as the systems existed, it was they who took decisions, and not my parents. As a matter of fact, I saw my parents too consult them. That could be how I learnt to respect professionals very early on.

Even today, in our organisations, professionals are respected and given their due place. Decision-making happens in equanimity and after consultation with respective professionals who are experts in their areas of specialisations.

Another important thing I learnt was self-discipline. While one fails to understand the importance and necessity of this virtue as a child, only time and experience show how it is discipline that sets people apart. Discipline builds personality and character. It builds a sense of urgency and focus that helps in easing out of trying and tough situations. Along the way, you realise how well discipline can spin off several positive traits as well. Self-discipline helps you to analyse different options and figure out what's the best course available. The eyes of a child are often filled with wonderment, excitement and questioning. With me the questioning remained but the wonderment soon got replaced with hard and practical situations.

WHEN YOU ARE A ROYAL YOU DON'T NEED TO SAY IT, IT SHOWS. WHAT SETS YOU APART IN BEING ROYAL IS YOUR CONDUCT AND REGAL IN YOUR DEMEANOUR.

Exposure to the world beyond home makes it real – pains and gains, learning and earning, knowing and growing.

CHAPTER THREE

Believe And Take Lead

I do believe the base for everything in life is love. How well you are loved will define how well you love. How much you are cared for will decide how you learn to look after. How responsible someone is towards you will determine how well you learn accountability. What books can't teach, experience will. And what experience teaches, is learnt best. For the larger part of my life, I have figured that self-confidence plays a tremendous role in shaping your life and plans. It is the primary factor that builds your appetite to take risks and teaches you to never lose faith in yourself. While these learnings may seem repetitive, oft-heard and even straight out of books, these are tried and tested formulae that rarely fail when understood and implemented.

There have been defining elements that shaped me into a confident and driven young girl. I could make and own up choices; I knew what to embrace and what to give up. Growing up years were all about taking decisions, despite being a school-going girl myself; they were about learning on the job. Those days were also about questioning restrictions and being unaccepting of norms. Teenage years passed by soaking in life around, analysing and understanding everything acceptable, and figuring out what was next.

Confidence Driven

Of everything that builds you up, confidence and the feeling of being able is paramount. And where does it generate from? It comes from being deeply loved by your folks. I owe and attribute my life and achievements to loads of love from home. I grew up feeling like a princess in the true sense of the term. Being exceptionally popular at school was a great boost as well. While there were huge upheavals and challenges that life threw my way, the love I was showered with helped me stay rooted.

Having learnt the value of prayers and gratitude helped build pillars of continued support. The more the challenges and subsequent success, the better transformation prayers and gratitude can provide to a person of substance. But what truly keeps things in check is optimum doses of self-assurance and self-confidence.

If you are under-confident, you lose precious time due to internal conversations and various iterations before your plan flows right. With over-confidence, you are bound to err and appear brazen, something that isn't an alluring trait. However, if you are intuitively self-confident without making it a big deal or putting on airs about it, you can go about life doing the right things along with appropriate course correction if and when slip-ups occur.

Handling Finances Early

Very early on, I realised how important and critical it was to understand and take charge of finances. Whether at home or at work, finance has been the backbone. My days at Indian Institute of Management helped me hone my skills of understanding the macro management of finances. Since I began handling accounts at a very early age, I had a fairly appropriate understanding of money matters.

I understood that wealth was important, but it certainly wasn't everything; I understood that money was required to run a well-oiled home and later an organisation, but it was the people who were more important. Finance was integral but core values and a humanistic approach had greater significance.

Being a Woman

Much as you may want this to be a non-issue or an insignificant aspect, fact is on many occasions women have to fight it out – to prove themselves, to get work done, to be taken seriously. I have experienced this on many occasions professionally, beginning with the days when I was starting out, building Delhi Public School in Ahmedabad. I was in my twenties and realised that wearing jeans wasn't quite helping my image, hence I switched to wearing sarees. What's more, I would often wear spectacles to appear older. These may seem insignificant but they have a deep impact. Over the years, I have noted how the right get-up and an appropriate attitude helps. Likewise, in offices and organisations with a large workforce, there is a distinguishing factor where women, their dressing, their work timings and even promotions are concerned. Is there a difference in the way women are perceived? Does it make working tougher for them as compared to men? Perhaps yes, and this discrimination isn't recent. It has existed for ages, surprisingly not just in India, but the world over. Today, the way women are perceived in India and across the world may have progressed in some measure, but the comparison and divide definitely remain.

Rebel with a Cause

I remember I had a lot of questions regarding the restrictions that social norms put on the ladies of the house. I wondered why my mother had to stay in *purdah* while my father walked around freely in and outside the house, why there were separate male and female sections in the palace, why the males were completely restricted from entering the Rani Mahal wing. Why my brother enjoyed more freedom than me, why he could ride a bike but not me, were questions that rattled me. Why was it taken for granted that my brother would grow up and be responsible for the wellbeing of the family and not my sister or me? These thoughts kept buzzing in my head and honestly, I found no answers.

Did I turn rebellious in the process? Perhaps I did. I probably felt I could get my way by being so. Subconsciously, an obvious solution that struck me was to be tomboyish, maybe because it appeared as if male members had all the influence and authority. At least that is what it seemed at the outset. It was much later that I figured gender didn't quite matter where decision-making was concerned. There would be times I opposed plans and decisions that subjugated women; my first firm decision was to force my way into studying in a co-ed college since until then only all-girls' institutions were allowed for us. Another big decision I had a hand in was deciding my sister's wedding venue and other festivities even though I was barely seventeen. Even today, when I try to rationalise steps taken back then, there is a sense of having contributed to making a huge difference to mind-sets. Over the years, I have evolved from being a rebel to an individualistic person. It is quite the pendulum effect: when you start out, it swings to extremes but soon it settles down in the centre and becomes balanced.

Short Crop and Long Rides

I did have long hair but I never saw it as a symbol of feminine beauty. I do not agree with the way Indian history perceives and portrays women. Me deciding to cut my hair was a symbolic yet very profound statement since it wasn't permitted in our family. Long tresses were, as was believed since early times, a sign of prettiness, dignity and femininity. Certain moments of our life get etched in our memory; I distinctly recall the day I finished my last Board exam and went straight to the salon to have my hair cropped. Within minutes, the waist-length hair was up to the shoulder. It was my way of declaring to the world, 'I am in charge of my life.'

Another interest, if I may say so, was cycling. I took to riding on an impulse but it provided me with a great sense of freedom and filled me with immense joy. Those wheels were a source of happiness that I could turn to anytime; I would just pick up my bike and set off anywhere. Be it a ride to the school or my tuition classes, taking off on my bicycle was liberating, it was freedom that I cherished. While still in school, my friends would rely a lot on me and I would escort them on my bike. I would also run errands for teachers on the wheels. My bike, besides giving me a sense of freedom, also branded me as a reliable and dependable person and I have remained thus, all these years.

Another episode I recall is wearing jeans for the first time and subsequently thereon. I think I chose the attire to defy norms and customs. Girls were not allowed to wear trousers, and the reason behind such a restriction was beyond my comprehension. What perhaps may have begun as battling norms and meaningless illogical practices, turned into lifelong interests and habits. I love cycling as a sport and have had various memorable rides. And jeans remain my favourite attire to date.

Coming from a traditional background, from a family that was revered, it may come across as surprising how I broke norms so to say, or walked the unusual path. But even when I did that it was always in a spirit of fun. I had always been friendly and naughty, indulging in pranks whenever the opportunity arose. But I never exceeded my boundaries or did anything that would hurt my mother's sentiments. It is only after my mother passed away that I lived life on my own terms. And once I began to do that, there was no need to be a rebel anymore. Rebellion fell by the wayside.

Fashioned to Excel

I won't say I did not notice or appreciate fashion, but I never chased it. I have loved watching and wearing fabrics from across regions and platforms, greatly appreciated embroidery and handwork. I enjoyed watching fashion flourish around me, especially in my late teens. But to me, proving my worth as a 'girl born in a royal family' seemed more meaningful.

Moreover, I was always inclined to intellectual work. Having said that, let me state that the fashion and glamour industry is not in any way less challenging, but for me it wasn't the right option as it would have been frowned upon by my family. I was anyway taking a risk by stepping out of the house. Working in the glamour industry would have been a double whammy! And then, it wasn't something that really inspired me, though I distinctly remember the first few times my body structure attracted attention from the fashion world. As a teenager, I received quite a few modelling proposals. I remember being approached with modelling assignments while walking down Delhi's famous Connaught Place (now Rajiv Chowk). Somehow I was never really taken in by the glamour world.

Stepping Out and Beyond

Images and portrayals of women and femininity may have undergone a myriad changes down the ages, yet, even now, we are bound by the shackles of preconceived notions of how a woman is 'supposed' to be. My adopting changes or doing things my way was by no means an attempt to make things easier and neither did it happen that way. There was no plan or formula, and stereotypes don't always work. Women at work have to be tough in their demeanour and their thinking and this is something I figured very early on. The kind of gentleness expected of us in the royal family is not what professional women are made of. Women from royal families, who have stepped out of their comfort zones to embrace the professional world, have had to adapt themselves to the environment. Like it or not, it is a man's world and it seems women must adapt to coexist in the same space.

What's in a Name?

Come to think of it, a name is plainly an address, a means of associating with and identifying a person. My parents christened me Manjula Manjari Devi; my in-laws addressed me as Pooja. As per Gujarati tradition, where a woman adopts the husband's name I adopted my second name instead. In hindsight, I am glad for the foresight, or else in the virtual world, as it is today, if I became Pooja Pratul Shroff from Manjula Manjari Devi, no one would have been able to locate me. While I don't see it entirely as an issue, this practice of changing a woman's name surely can create confusion. I have often been asked if Manjula is my mother's name; since I come from the East, they assume that I would be carrying my mother's name. For the record, I simply tell people, Manjula Pooja (Shroff) is my name.

To be a rebel does not necessarily mean being a non-conformist. Often it is being a pioneer, seeking change and having the desire for individuality.

From a safe haven to brave the world and beyond, some changes mark a strength unseen. Childhood bliss and learning mingle in harmony.

CHAPTER FOUR

Cradled In A Hostel

For reasons unfathomable, school days remain special and memorable throughout our lifetime.

My early childhood days were spent under the warm and loving umbrella of a nurturing family. Though I was still very young, those early memories – fun with friends, long play hours, mindless chatter, carefree times – are still contained somewhere in the deep recesses of my mind. The comfort of everyday living, if not necessarily taken for granted, becomes a habit you somehow get used to. And then, there comes a change. Like it did in my case. I was sent to a hostel at a very young age and today, when I look back, I realise it was one of the firming chapters of my life.

Responsibilities tend to make you accountable; they give you a direction and a goal, whatever be the magnitude. In my case, if not for the early responsibilities, I probably wouldn't have turned out the way I am. I may not have had the confidence that I otherwise have gained, and who knows, the ability to make plans, steer them to fruition, and to take lead wouldn't have been the same. Unknowingly, my early life, filled with immense responsibilities, has had a tremendous role in shaping my personality.

The sense of ownership towards tasks I undertake got instilled in me at a very young age. At a time when others were only juggling homework and play, I had quite a field to engage in. I believe I am wired to stay enthusiastic, no matter what; this has made me willingly take up responsibilities, something I never shirked. And, whatever I undertook, my unflinching dedication to it was always complete.

It is very early that I understood a task isn't big or small, significant or insignificant, the task itself is paramount; how we carry it out is what matters. I never thought jobs were done to please others. As a result, I acquired a straightforward and no apple-polishing method of working. If there was a task at hand, it had to be attended to. I had a direct approach to my work which kept me away from any form of politics and strategies that encourage either unfair practices or shortcuts to achieve targets.

From Home to Hostel

I faintly remember leisurely waking up at home, birds chirping on my favourite tree, the sun peeping in through windows and doors, filling the rooms with positivity and cheer as only nature can manage. Breakfasts, lunches and dinners were mini feasts; since we were children, care was taken to give us healthy food, but it was always delicious. Life at home was pretty much blissful with mother's affection showered liberally on us.

But soon that came to an end. Before long, I found myself in a hostel. And once in, no excuses were permitted. There was no one to listen to your complaints; nobody to pamper or soft pedal issues for you. All in all, there was a no-nonsense approach and attitude to everything and we had to understand that crisp and clear. While initial days were full of wonder and misgivings, I later realised that this approach to life is very necessary. I am not sure if everyone must experience hostel life at the age of five, the way I did, but I strongly feel everyone must at some point in their lives get to stay away from home, at least during later years or during college life, to learn what independence is. Not only that, hostel life also teaches you to be responsible, self-reliant, to co-exist and adjust with others.

Being from a royal family, my sister and I somehow got slightly preferential treatment. We were easily recognised and allowed to celebrate festivals. Apart from friends who were regular classmates, there were several girls from other royal families as well, and we bonded well. A cousin, who was about six or seven years older, would look out for me and similarly I would watch out for younger distant cousins. Somewhere each one was connected to the other through families and extended relations.

A Training Ground

Introvert, extrovert, ambivert, whatever you may inherently be, life at a hostel teaches you to make friends and bond with others. It lets you experience the joy of trusting, the ability to do something for others, rely on them and let them feel the same for you. You learn to share, not just things and spaces, but thoughts, ideas and feelings too. In the process, I feel, you become empathetic towards others, and understand what they are going through. In fact, the art of bonding and friendship comes naturally in hostels. Learning to help each other, cooperate, as well as have healthy competition – it is all inculcated in a hostel over time. Hostel life also fosters real inter-personal relationships that come in handy in later years, in our profession and career.

One of the biggest takeaways for me has been emotional independence. Staying at a hostel since a very young age taught me self-reliance of the highest order. I knew I had to do it for myself, that there was no person, no parent, no entourage to support me when it came to daily activities and goings-on. Early experiences tend to impact in deeper ways since those are impressionable formative years; they tend to leave a mark and influence your thoughts, notions and psychology. Even today, after all these years and experiences, I rely and lean on my inner self rather than on the outside world.

Skills and School

There was consistency as far as the approach to education and the takeaways from it were concerned. From inception to my Board exams, I was in the same school and therefore I have no comparisons to make as far as the process or the result is concerned. But judging by the fact that nearly 20 per cent of my batch mates chose Education as a career, the school surely did something right for all of us.

Good values were stressed upon. We were made to appreciate that kindness and compassion were fundamental building blocks. My love for the English language, reading, sports, and oration took root and blossomed there. My school life has been one of the best phases of my life, a period I can take a peep into for that feel-good factor. There are times I look back only to strongly feel that my school sowed the right seeds and showed me how critical education is to societal development. It is this lingering residual thought that perhaps got me involved and then engrossed in contributing to societal transformation through education. It is the realisation that good schooling can work wonders in not just educating you and preparing you for a career but also in shaping your life in such a manner that you find meaning in your moves and strength to pursue your ambitions.

The Irish Convent Stamp

Studying at a convent is known to instil certain qualities in you, the key ones being strong mettle and sound character. I enjoy remembering those childhood days, those early hostel and school times, when everything was methodical, conventional and formal. However, certain aspects of convent life have simply become a part of me, the daily prayer being one. The practice of daily prayer is something I follow till date.

The rules in the convent were meant to be adhered to; there was no questioning, no debate, no pleading. It was *the* way of life and something meant to be absorbed with grace. Being prim and proper was another principal virtue at the convent. Being shabby and indecorous was not an option and simply unheard of. However, what I will always be grateful for is the grooming I received as a young lady, to understand the value of being dignified in all circumstances. No matter what life throws at you, how you deal with it, the grace and dignity is what talks of your breeding. I learned there was no alternative to refinement; that was the only way to be, no matter what the circumstance.

School Friends are Forever

The world is richer owing to friends; there is rarely a soul who would disagree with this. Our lives are richer because of friendships, bonds that are based on deep trust and understanding and those that give pure joy.

While I was in school and college, staying in touch with friends happened largely through letters, if at all. There were no emails or social media platforms to connect on and stay in touch then. But the world has undergone a massive shift in the past couple of decades and I found myself in touch with my entire class once again. In fact, a few years ago, I started a WhatsApp group of batch mates, and within a matter of days, we managed to locate everyone. As many as forty-two of us are regularly in touch and keep up with the goings-on in each other's lives. Did I think this possible when I passed out of school? Could I have imagined something like this even a decade ago? Not quite, but technology has been delightfully responsible for getting friends and close ones together on a common platform. Today, when some are settled abroad, we have a worldwide group and keep in touch through this medium, which we never ever imagined we'd have.

Being 'Florence Nightingale'

School days were full of memorable experiences and incidents, some of which have been life altering in many ways. Certain incidents taught important lessons while some experiences stood out for their significant nature. I remember being called

Florence Nightingale by some due to my diligent social services. The school had adopted Shishu Bhawan, a children's hospital, where we would routinely clean hospitals beds, toilets and take care of terminally ill young children. Right next to the school was Daya Ashram, an old age home, a place where we spent hours attending to the elderly. I have volunteered in countless cataract eye camps and mobile leprosy clinics.

I come from a feudal home that practices social hierarchy. And that makes me recall an exceptional incident where once a servant of our home joined Daya Ashram and I actually tended to her needs as a volunteer. This helped me break down social hierarchy and introduced in me the value of treating all people as equal. I have always questioned inequality, if not on large open platforms, at least within my circle of people and related systems. My compassion and need to serve society pretty much originated in my school days.

From Feeling Homesick to Playing Pranks

I clearly remember enjoying vacations at home to the fullest and then going back to the hostel with a heavy heart. But this lasted only for the first few weeks. We had two vacations a year, one during summer and the other during Christmas. For the first few days after returning, I would be very homesick, but since my sister was in the same hostel, I would re-adjust and bounce back in just a few days. I would get back to my classes and games, homework and pranks, all of these happening side by side.

I must admit, I was easily the naughtiest girl in class (from the Enid Blyton series) but it was always about having clean, safe fun. Not only was I tremendously popular, I was equally loved by my teachers. There was never any manipulation, malice or harm in my pranks, only playful acts like bunking homework, skipping afternoon siesta, climbing trees, hiding and chatting in the bathroom in the middle of the night, eating snacks at midnight after the tuck shop closed for the day. Who knew these would make for cherished memories later.

Leading the Way

Every year, I was assigned a leadership and supervisory role in school. By the time I reached high school, I had been a dorm monitor, house monitor, class monitor, afternoon siesta check monitor, cupboards in-charge, mess in-charge, house and sports captain.

Ah, these titles meant a lot at school; the responsibility they entailed would ensure maturity and ability to handle challenging situations with élan. That apart, it encouraged to indulge in good past times, reading being one. I pretty much enjoyed reading, from Enid Blyton's *Secret Seven* and *Famous Five* to *Malory Towers*, *Naughtiest Girl series*, to Thomas Hardy and Mills and Boons. Reading creates a beautiful world, some consider it an escape while others relish the sense of belongingness it evokes. I have seen books as friends and companions and also as guides and masters. I have seen books change lives – for the better, for the go-getter.

TO BE BORN IN PLENTY IS SHEER LUCK, TO BECOME ONE WHO CAN GIVE PLENTY IS GOOD FATE. AND WHAT YOU GIVE, YOU GET BACK IN ABUNDANCE.

Leaving home is never easy, neither is charting a course. Eagerness and resolution, along the path, leads you on.

CHAPTER FIVE

Homing In...

Leaving places where your story began is truly tough, for you always leave a piece of yourself behind. The branches of the tree may spread far and wide, the flowers may bloom still further away but the plant forever remains connected to the roots. That more or less explains how little bits of our childhood, upbringing, learning and experiences of early years, translate into hopeful and achievable tomorrows. Our early days, our past never quite leaves us. It becomes the mould that shapes our days to come. It is the yesterday that encourages the tomorrow, although today is where the action is.

Odisha got me to Delhi but Ahmedabad is what happened along the way. I often look back to figure out and connect the dots, and while in hindsight it seems smooth how one connected with the other, it actually happened owing to the choices made and decisions taken. For me, Delhi is where life happened. It is a place that has my heart; it is a city that shaped me into what I am today; it is where I grew; it is where life offered me directions, bold and new.

Understanding Freedom

Leaving Odisha for Delhi meant moving from one world to another completely different one; it meant stepping out of a cosy cocoon for an unknown territory. It also meant freedom tagged with responsibility after living a very secluded and sheltered life back home. I had never travelled by myself, never stepped out alone, and always had people chaperone me. In comparison to that, it was a different world I found myself in, one where I was always commuting alone with only my thoughts for company. I would often reminisce about the little two-ponytailed girl that I was, someone who hadn't travelled alone for nearly twenty years of her life, but was suddenly doing a lot of it. Images from childhood and even the recent past, when I was in my late teens, would flash across my mind, reminding me how far I had come. And that was only the beginning… today, I have travelled alone and seen a good part of the world by myself.

But I often relive the feeling I had felt back then, of travelling distances alone, all the while being responsible for nothing but the self. To me it was some sort of liberation as well. In fact, so many things meant freedom to me. Picking and choosing vegetables from a vendor was freedom; purchasing my travel tickets was too. Searching for a job was freedom and so was enrolling in a co-ed programme. Small and apparently insignificant things that most people tend to take for granted meant so much to me. It was an unmatched thrill, be it mundane chores or simple everyday activities.

Looking Back

Some incidents change you forever. They weaken or strengthen you, depending on their immediacy, time and situation. They result in a permanent change within, and hence in your outlook towards life. My mother doted on me. Losing her in my early twenties, and that too suddenly, was an extremely traumatic experience. It took me several years to come to terms with the loss, to accept that she was gone from this world that millions inhabit, that she was physically missing from my world. The anguish and deep sorrow following her death is something I carried within for a very long time. Strangely, however, there was also a feeling of being free. I felt I was suddenly not answerable to anyone anymore.

Somewhere I realised, I would have to live on my own terms and shape my life in a way my mother would be proud of. I wanted to do something meaningful; this desire often drove me from one step to another. I wanted to prove my worth and be everything that my mother could not be. She was like a beautiful porcelain doll, kept inside a palace, meant only to follow, never to lead or take tough decisions. Somewhere that generated the strength and drive in me to go out there in the world and live a real life, one that was in sharp contrast to hers.

Blood Ties

There is a strange thing about being alone and nursing a desire to prove something. While there is an inner confidence, there is also a deep desire to connect with your immediate folks, those you know will give you the boost, encourage or simply hear you out. It was my sister who I would keep in touch with back home when I moved to Delhi. I did have plenty of relatives but we were more of a small nuclear family, and with both parents passing away at an early age, there was just us siblings, the three of us, who were there for each other. My sister was the only one I kept in touch with since I was very concerned about her facing social pressure back in Odisha after I left. My brother, on the other hand, would not understand the need for me to toil it out in Delhi, all by myself, only to prove my worth. Somehow being in touch with my sister gave me a feeling of belonging too, which at that point I really needed since I was alone in a new world amid people I didn't know.

A New Way of Life

From high palace walls to a terrace room that wasn't entirely mine, Delhi was an eye-opener in every sense. As it is, the first few days in a new city are never easy. To top it, I remember feeling surprised much too often – at myself, and at how life could change, suddenly and drastically. I lived in a *barsaati* in Delhi, which is typically a terrace room accommodation that a family living in a bungalow rents out. From a palace to a barsaati sounds quite a mammoth adjustment but interestingly it wasn't so for me. I was on top of the world, all eager to set out and make my mark.

In the barsaati, there were some friends from college also; they had been living in a hostel in Delhi, until we all decided to stay together. It sure was loads of fun to live with friends but it was not easy by any stretch of the imagination. From living in comfort at home to trying and creating it for myself day by day, it was like experiencing and living through some series of a 'step-by-step guide to independent living'.

I remember walking the roads of Delhi, watching buildings

and people go by, with a fire burning within me that kept me going. It is this inner mettle that goaded me, reminded me that I was born to make a difference, that I must find my path. It was my source of strength, the inner motivation that drove me to excel.

At all times, there was only one primary thought: I have to prove myself. Despite all odds, I had ventured out to create a life of my own and failure was simply not an option. Starting off wasn't easy; it involved basic jobs like cleaning the space I lived in, washing clothes, cooking on a gas stove, sleeping in the terrace room in the bitter Delhi winters with only a second hand heater for comfort, commuting by DTC buses, job hunting. From the life I had lived and known, this seemed pretty rough and tough but I never regretted anything. All those days of hardship built me into what I am today. I can work in any condition, and I never shy away from hard work. I truly believe you have to be the smartest and the most hardworking person in the room, that you have no choice but to be at the top of your game. And if you work towards your goal with absolute dedication, there is no way success won't hug you hard.

Friendships and Influences

New places create a wide open space for you to fill – with ideas, experiences and people. Those initial days in Delhi involved a lot of learning, independent living and interactions that paved the way further. I was like a sponge soaking in everything I came across. I met some very good people who shaped the way I think, those who were instrumental in holding my hand and teaching me. They showed me the path to success. Those few years catapulted my capabilities and my understanding of the world. I learnt and unlearnt, I struggled and I got better. It was that home ground that prepared me for who I am today.

Braving Life

Quiet moments allow you to think, to mull over steps you have taken, face consequences and own up decisions. When I landed in Delhi, the idea was to prove myself but there was no plan in place and it surely wasn't a cakewalk. A case in point could be using the public transport; it definitely wasn't easy since I had never done it before. Delhi is a rough city for women commuters. It is here that I learnt the art of self-protection. I remember carrying a pepper spray and would never hesitate to raise my voice or confront someone if I felt something amiss, be it for myself or fellow women commuters. If something was wrong, I believed in addressing it rather than ignoring and moving away. The lessons of self-protection and self-preservation are deep set in me. The sense of being careful and cautious in new places, being safe rather than sorry is something I carry with me till date. While these are things you learn as you face challenging situations and times, how you react has a lot to do with how you have been brought up, how you have been treated, as well as your sense of right and wrong.

Embracing Change

I was on the threshold of change. Now, it was my turn to allow it to mould me, teach me and hone me. I worked hard and lost that last bit of childishness that was so characteristic of me during all my growing up years. I realised it was time for a change, a leap, and in the process, there would be certain things I would leave behind and some others I might need to embrace. I began to focus on building a career and my risk-taking appetite increased as well. I started to observe things minutely and assess them. It was like a study of sorts, which in the long run, has helped me gain perspective and sharpened my acumen. None but myself would have to take decisions and own up consequences, I told myself clearly. In the process, some decisions would be right, others may not strike so well, and yet you must move on keeping intact your positive spirit. In the entire process of this life-changing transition, I also realised that the absence of pampering can make one stronger since there is no false sense of support to fall back on. You know, there is only one way and that is the way ahead. I was aware I could meet with failure but I would learn from mistakes, fall, get up, learn and move forward. Failure leads you to success if you are a willing learner. I fell along the way, but each time I fell, it was forward. I kept failing and falling forward; the only place I looked towards was ahead, never behind.

In Delhi, I Found Home...

Delhi has been my first real home. Even today I consider myself a Delhiite above everything else. I spent my formative years in Odisha, then moved to Delhi and then to Gujarat; by now I think I have spent an equivalent period in all these places. Delhi grew me as a professional. It is in this city that I took risks and started my company; I found myself hiring people, learning the ropes of the corporate ladder, as well as getting statutory work done. There were so many learning opportunities I got in Delhi; I met people from diverse backgrounds and regions, and realised how driven most of them were.

I have long been in Gujarat now, but Delhi is still close to my heart. I will always see the city as the one that taught me ambition and self-preservation, it taught me to solve problems and think clearly. Delhi gave me happiness and taught me to deal with sorrow, it gave me friends and made me mature. 'You can take a person out of Delhi, but you cannot take Delhi out of a person,' is a popular quote. I couldn't subscribe to this more now than I ever have. Delhi stays within.

It tends to go unnoticed that strong people can get tired of being strong.

You receive it well, hence you give it better. Situations and people don't change, it is love and affection that makes all the difference.

CHAPTER SIX

Bonds Of Love

The nods you received and the attention you were showered with, the importance you were given and the affection you grew rich with, nothing from childhood is ever past recollection. Experiences from early days leave lasting impressions. They go on to direct and often shape the tomorrows.

Every time I wonder about the way I behave, the opinions I have, my belief systems, I realise they have a lot to do with the love and importance I received as a child.

Besides key family members, there are always a set of friends who invariably end up impacting our lives and thoughts. Some are comfort providers, a few are sounding boards and then there are some who simply enhance our life by being a part of it. They add to the laughter and reduce stress, they partake in our sorrows and enrich us with their company. These friends are ongoing influences. And then, there is the love of a child.

Nothing ever comes close to it; nothing perhaps ever will. The love children give has powers to change so much – from ideas and notions to interests and lifestyle. Family, friends, love and fondness, there is a lot that builds itself around these.

What is Love?

It may be a small word but it is a broad term. Love is eternal, and true to the adage, love indeed makes the world go round. When you give and receive it, you believe everything is possible. It injects positivity and the confidence of being able to achieve practically anything. With love in your heart, you can even win over adversaries. It may sound glorified, but love is quite the solution to every problem there is in life. It is so broad and so all-encompassing that words don't justify its power and effect. Interestingly, while it is the most favoured emotion across the world, it is also one that cannot always be guided by reason. Love can be blind, as is believed by more than half the world, and it does not consider shape, size, caste, creed or colour. Love is unpredictable and perhaps the one emotion that can drive you to any extent.

A powerful emotion, love can only be experienced to know what it truly feels like. It is also a very strong emotion and hence if things were to unfortunately turn sour, as it happens at times, people end up becoming enemies. That is indeed a regrettable and sad aspect, since if you delve deeper, you understand that pure love is a healing agent, not something that breaks or destroys you.

I have always viewed love in a very broad way. I love humanity at large and serve it with utmost selflessness. I am a giver who loves bringing smiles on people's faces. It gives me immense joy; it evokes a feeling of having accomplished something meaningful. Over the years, I have honed my giving skills. I am not afraid of giving and believe there is enough in this universe to support me and everyone else.

Self-Made with Love

Haven't we all grown up knowing that love is the cure for all misery? It teaches you so much, it inspires and leads you to achievements you never envisaged. It drives you to chase your desires, at the same time pushing you towards your goals. Love for the self or self-love, as it is popularly termed, is not just a motivator but also the very foundation from where things arise and move forward.

I am a self-made person, aware that self-made people are by and large hungry to learn from everything around, be they situations, people or places. I have learnt from people I have worked for, as also from those who worked for me. I have absorbed and learnt from circumstances, from pleasant situations and a lot from unpleasant ones too. And while life can throw a mixed bag of experiences for you to deal with, I believe love for self makes you stride through everything, though preservation of optimism, beliefs and ideas is a prerequisite. My life has been very rich in experiences of every kind, and I have welcomed and dealt with a variety of episodes with utmost care, for the cause as well as for the self.

Bonds that Let You Soar

When people have faith in you, you are confident of being on track and assured of walking the right path. And should you stumble at some point, there is a reassuring voice within that tells you there is support. Consistent backing gives a positive feeling which allows a person to soar. Today I am grateful, I have been a well-loved person. In my formative years, I was always surrounded by people who loved me. Over the years, I have realised that I have received immense love at every step of my life. My mother simply adored me; from my uncles and aunts, my siblings, my in-laws – there was always an abundance of affection flowing towards me all through my life.

School, too, has been a motivating force. My principal, teachers and friends have been positive influences. Early age is an interesting and deciding factor in terms of shaping your ideas of love and friendship, building self-esteem and motivation to pursue what is desirable.

As time goes by, you realise how love in various forms makes you a wholesome person, willing to both give and receive. You are more compassionate, more understanding. But that does not need to clash with how you demand work. At work, I am an extremely demanding person, thorough and clear about all that is to be done, but I haven't seen that come in the way of people's love and affection towards me. I receive tremendous amount of love at work too, and am grateful for it.

There is always an unseen and unspoken chord that binds people together whether the relationship is personal, professional or even general. Some can be explained and elaborated upon, some simply cannot be. Likewise, some bonds result in pushing us to do the best in circumstances, while some teach us to sit back and deal with what comes by. I have always tried not to let hierarchy come in the way of people's suggestions. I am neither stubborn about listening to people, nor do I discard their suggestion if it seems to infringe upon my freedom. Since I make decisions and choose options with clarity of mind, I value people's feedback, be it regarding work or on the personal front, as it could be coming from genuine concern. I listen with an open heart and mind and realise the point that is being conveyed, along with the emotion and intent it comes with. Irrespective of whether you follow what is told to you, the art of listening and absorbing goes a long way in making one's own life sorted and peaceful.

Friends are a Blessing

Friends are by choice, unlike certain relationships that come with clauses and expectations, misgivings or baggage. Friends are those bonds that help you sail through tough times, those that add to your daily dose of joy. Having friends who you can absolutely trust and rely upon is a direct gift from heaven.

There are some close friends I can trust my life with; life wouldn't be the same without them around. I have also seen how friends shape you along the way – their thoughts, ideas and suggestions often make it through to you. From time to time, I have received critical appraisals and feedbacks from friends that have gone a long way in developing me and making me who I am.

Home Beyond Home

School and family gatherings are where we make our first few friends. The reasons for bonding are innocent: liking the same game, finding similar things funny, laughing over practically nothing, or playing together endlessly. As one grows, it is hobbies and varied interests that bring people together. And, with time, you realise if there's anyone you'd implicitly trust beyond family, it is your friends. That is how significant their impact is, how comfortable their company is. While I had pretty much the same friends throughout my school days, especially at the hostel, life was waiting to change when I got to Delhi.

Delhi is a big city and it is not so easy to start a life there. Besides, it has always been known to be unsafe for women. You have to be on guard while meeting new people and transacting with them. My life before reaching the capital city was a total contrast. I had had a sheltered protected life, and the first few days in Delhi made me realise I was out in a big, wide world. It was due to the support of close friends that I was able to carve a life for myself there. Often, when I look back and think of my early days, I am reminded of my barsaati mates and the people in Delhi University, North Campus where I worked. My organisation Kalorex first took shape in Delhi and I have good memories of the people I worked with when we started out there, be it their enthusiasm and knowledge or support and willingness to back me up.

Love Begins with a Mother

There will possibly never be a love greater than a mother's. When you rear a child and pour yourself into making motherhood the best experience of your life, it has to be special. When you care for someone more than you ever thought it was possible to care for someone, it becomes magical. When nothing seems to be going right and yet you don't give up, it is for a love that is eternal.

The reason why a mother's love assumes such significant proportions is because it is the source of everything. Mother is the first real relationship a child has and this source-relationship defines the way the child is going to grow up; it determines the way the child as an adult will conduct other relationships. Those who have a dysfunctional relationship with their mother are more likely to have aspects of dysfunctionality in their relationships as adults. On the other hand, those who have been loved and looked after in a manner both indulgent and mindful, are comfortable with their expressions of love, and are at ease when dealing with people they love and care for.

Unassuming, undemanding, forever giving and selfless, that is what a mother-child relationship actually is. And while it is understood to be the epitome of love, it is perhaps the only bond that cannot be boxed into a category, simply because it is unending, everlasting and has vast variations. Indeed, blessed are those who have tight bonds with their mothers.

While my love for my mother and some other immediate relationships was immense, my earliest memories of love are also associated with pain. I lost a lot of important people I loved dearly while growing up, and that caused quite a bit of trauma. That, unfortunately, is the power of love. It is so intense; just as it makes you, it breaks you too.

Are Marriages Made in Heaven?

Why one decides to get married and to whom – there need not be one specific reason. It could be an instant decision driven by instinct, it could also be one led by feelings, or as most would have us believe, it happens because 'marriages are made in heaven'.

I would say I have had a pretty unconventional marriage which many people may find not only unusual but hard to comprehend. It has come with all the trappings of modern contemporary marriages – inter-caste, long distance, different priorities, etcetera.

But whether it was the biggest of decisions like the freedom to choose my career or the smallest decision like deciding what to eat next, I have enjoyed unbridled freedom in my marriage. I have received tremendous support and trust from family members when chips have been down. I have been privileged to receive unconditional support and help, be it tangible or intangible, which has helped in better dealing of future courses. The Shroff family's value system of integrity, honesty of purpose, and a straightforward, simple approach to life is extremely laudable.

Every marriage has a purpose, a path. Marriage is also a great teacher; it teaches you some of life's major lessons. Since relationships are complex in nature, maintaining a marriage provides insights into the handling, nurturing and growth of relationships. Also, as one navigates through the twists and turns of life, family provides a sense of comfort, a sense of ease. There are several times in life's journey when one wonders how one was led to where one is, and except connecting the dots, there is little else that provides an answer. Perhaps that is why it is said, marriages are made in heaven!

The Love of a Child

Adults tend to think and presume that they are the ones teaching children the values of love and respect, togetherness and loyalty. But like many others, I too was in for a surprise when I realised how much I had learnt about love from my son, when I realised it was he who made me understand what love truly is.

It is amazing how much children can teach you. When he was very young, I learnt to act in complete accordance with my speech. I noticed how he would mirror even the slightest disconnect. In the days when he was growing up, I tried to become the person I wished for him to grow up as. My temper tantrums reduced and became almost non-existent; I definitely did not want my child to pick that up from me. My carefree approach and carelessness transformed into focus and responsibility since I wanted to be the right role model at work. I was gradually not only noticing the changes in me but was also noting how everything could alter and change only so that the child had a smooth, sound and balanced upbringing. There were moments I reflected upon, and realised the extent to which we are willing to go for love; how this love can completely turn our lives for the better, into an egoless state, and magically so.

I knew he would notice me and either behave similarly or at least do as I did. Actions speak louder than words, don't they? Now as an adult, he is wise enough to give me advice and does not hesitate in speaking his mind.

Along the way, I also discovered my ability to be non-judgmental and accept people the way they are. My sense of duty and loyalty sharpened as I took up responsibilities for my siblings and my in-laws. While essaying different roles teaches a lot about expectations you may have from those you care for, it is only when you love a child that you realise 'love is giving without expecting'. And it is this feeling that is sublime.

Life's expectations change from wanting the best to happen,

to accepting that
whatever happens,
happens for the best.

It is here that I have transformed lives, in the process, altering mine. It is here that I sought to learn, and destiny led me home.

CHAPTER SEVEN

Ahmedabad, Eventually

I believe ultimately it is not 'we' who make the plans; we are just a 'part' of it. If that sounds confusing, my Cuttack to Delhi to Ahmedabad journey might seem so too. But there is a larger plan that leads us to where we are meant to be. Ahmedabad, in hindsight, was waiting in the wings, to take me in its fold for the long run.

Being a working professional in Delhi, I was learning various aspects of business establishment and management. Somewhere, along the way, I was convinced theoretical study could accelerate my learning curve. The promising gates of Indian Institute of Management welcomed me and destiny, as time would reveal, made plans to keep me there. As I went about building a career, it also got clearer that management lessons were essential. And why just me, I believe management studies are a must for everyone; they should be the foundation for any professional degree. At the institute, days soon turned to months and the classroom got familiar. Case studies and theories, thinking and execution, these increasingly became part of my days.

The First Lessons

Once I was at the institute with dedicated time for learning and studying, my involvement was absolute. Of the many things I learnt at IIMA, the key points were that there are no absolute rights or wrongs, though consequences of decisions one takes are their to face. Problem solving method and decision tree are imperative to create a scientific approach to any decision-making, and that, once the decision is taken, action points score over self-doubts. I also figured that mid-way assessments and feedbacks are necessary for course correction, if and when required.

Another vital aspect seemed understanding the importance of creating a strong culture and value system besides learning a host of technical lessons including financial forecasting and beyond. My problem-solving skills were well-honed here and financial acumen was sharpened; case-study methods drove home the point better and I found myself in the groove of learning and absorbing newer methodology.

And then, as a relief, there was the Louis Kahn Plaza…the iconic exposed brick campus, which is integral and connects to many an inspirational story. You see, ideas take birth there.

Making Ahmedabad Home

A city once world famous for its cotton textiles and mills and ever so popular for the tourist-friendly Sabarmati Ashram (home to Mahatma Gandhi for over a decade in the early 1900s), the city of Ahmedabad held a different meaning for me when I got here. It was the city where I sought to pursue management lessons before going back to Delhi and implementing my learning in the projects I undertook. While it's true I loved the IIMA campus and all that I learnt there, I had no inkling that it would hold me back. That Ahmedabad would turn into my *karmabhoomi*, a place I would call home, is something that was beyond contemplation.

I met Pratul at the institute and marriage with him started a new chapter. Like most big changes can be, this wasn't envisaged or planned. One thing led to another. In good time, I figured out how to execute what lay in the recesses of my mind... so, it is in Ahmedabad that I got to realise my dreams of providing education and transforming lives.

Destiny's Pick

We are led to where we are meant to be. Being a believer in the cosmic pattern and looking towards the bigger and higher purpose of life, I believe there are no coincidences. Whatever happens, is meant to be. Once I stepped into this city, I put my best foot forward to build a solid career. Post marriage, I would shuttle between Ahmedabad and Delhi; it was literally about spending half a month here and the other half there. Though after Advait was born, I ensured I considered doing only day trips.

The Gujarati Charm

Growing up in Odisha, quite the other end, I was enamoured by Gujarat, obviously with no inkling that life would eventually take me there. I remember having a couple of Gujarati friends in school and it was always delightful visiting their homes. In fact, I relished Gujarati food long before I set foot here; I found celebration of festivals unique and involving. Today, years later, I am a *pucca* Gujju, as we are fondly called. I enjoy the traditions, the sumptuous food spread, the simplicity of the people, the variety of festivals, the soul stirring music and the resplendent art. It is interesting how the city has strong roots in culture and people take pride in their literature and theatre. Be it the 'world famous' Ahmedabad traffic sense, the must-have street food, the penchant for celebrating every festival or occasion, and of course the passionate attachment to food and eateries that dot the city's scape – all of these make for a distinctive Amdavadi experience.

Fun and frolic apart, the matter-of-fact and unassuming approach of people in Gujarat is very charming. But something would be seriously amiss without an elaborate and fancy mention of *garba.* I am such a passionate garba enthusiast, people refuse to believe I am not a native Gujarati when they see me dance. In fact, garba time in this state is something one has to experience to even understand the madness and glory surrounding this most loved and looked-forward-to festival. From late night binge eating to hopping restaurants after a good garba spin, the magic of socialising and feasting is heightened around Navratri. It clearly can't get dreamier.

Honing Business Skills

Gujaratis have an acumen for business and the risk-taking appetite is definitely higher in this state given its long history in share market trading. For that matter, it is difficult to even teach vocational skills to people, for even semi-urban people are not too inclined to take up jobs. Students anyway are only interested in getting successful in a short span and believe it can happen only by building an enterprise. There seems to be a risk-taker in every home. I believe the environment of Ahmedabad, the entrepreneurial spirit of this city, made me a serial entrepreneur. When I started out, I would have been happy and content to have made some meaningful contributions with one school. I definitely had not dreamt of building tens of schools or reaching out to thousands and lakhs of people.

There is a lot I owe to the spirit and environment, both inside my home and outside in the professional work space, which was conducive to this sprawling growth. Along the way, I learnt to be simple, direct and straightforward. The Delhi work culture is slightly different, a tad pompous. I propagate simplicity and directness at work, avoid getting into complexities and discourage groupism. And each of these are in practice here at Kalorex, which has distributed leadership.

Education vis-à-vis Business

Call it a strange mix, but on the one hand, the business community does not quite value education the way the professional class does, and yet, Ahmedabad boasts of some of the most premier institutions in the Asia-Pacific map.

From all these years in education, I do hope I have added my bit to the already rich educational landscape of the city. Some data points show that schooling in Ahmedabad became more contemporary with the advent of the kind of schools we initiated. The eco-system of education became more fertile, encouraging many more institutions to come up.

Pearls of Wisdom

Work-life is known to be a great leveller, teaching you a lot more than you ever expected. Perhaps the reason is that most people you work with are unknown to you and as time passes, there are things you learn for your larger benefit. One of the most important lessons I have learnt is, there should be no emotions at work. Being objective and value-oriented are equally important, and having a fair and impartial approach is bound to lead you through a variety of ups and downs that work-life is anyway going to throw your way.

Message in a Brand

Besides impacting lakhs of people over two decades, I am a witness to some heart-warming cases where children from our NGO Visamo Kids have got into medical colleges, into top engineering institutions through JEE, into National Institute of Design and other colleges in that league. These are premier professional courses of India and obviously students from Below Poverty Line do not stand a chance at these prestigious institutes. Visamo Kids Foundation has been a gratifying project which has transformed the lives of many students. The need to have a shelter home was identified post the Gujarat earthquake in 2001 and that is when the Foundation was created. It selects children of merit and ensures they receive the best schooling and living standard. There are some heart-touching and exceptional stories of children who excelled owing to sheer talent, enthusiasm and quest for learning, all under the Foundation's umbrella.

Be it mainstream education or teaching students with special needs, providing equal opportunities to socially and economically backward children or providing international education to the affluent, Kalorex has been a forerunner. By due efforts and the grace of God, these have stayed a constant. What is a brand if it cannot make a change? What is a name if it cannot create an impact?

WHEN YOU ARE DESTINY'S CHILD AND ARE LED TO THE LIGHT AHEAD OF YOU, YOU ARE DETERMINED AND READY TO WORK HARD WITH NOTHING TO STALL YOUR WAY.

If nothing, there is the wealth of learning and education. Armed with purpose, will and resolution, the entrepreneurial drive takes off.

CHAPTER EIGHT

Education Above All

To seekers, every passing day of their life is richer owing to experience. There's some learning from every situation, some lesson from setbacks too. But what gives direction to the experience and knowledge acquired is education and all that comes with it. Thirst for education is known to have led the world towards goals that seemed unachievable, but intention has shown them the light of day. I have always given immense importance to early education, right from the time I was in school myself. Somehow the idea of studying was interwoven with achieving. And, that seems to have made all the difference.

First in Line

Since time immemorial, education has been the backbone of societal transformation. A distinguisher of right and wrong, it has helped build perspectives for people across generations.

Over the years, education has also undergone transformation to suit the continuous changing needs of society. Moving from the *guru-shishya parampara* to a regimented system of mass education, from student-centric approach to technology-driven methods, teaching and learning have witnessed sweeping changes. However, what has not changed is the impact education can have on a person.

A formidable education and the need to be a continuous learner are the most important assets, no matter what the circumstances may be. The inner channelling of the way you think, how you internalise your thoughts and behave, shapes you over the course of your life. Also, how you digest power and success is an indicator of education, likewise, how you hold ground, when the chips are down, explains how education has been processed. Education today is considered textual, exam-driven and marks-based but to me it is about shaping the individual.

Character above All

Nothing is as powerful as strength of character. This has been an oft-repeated line for us in our growing up years. A person's thinking abilities are impacted by education, it being a constructive and powerful tool for human advancement. However, character is the innermost attribute of a person. The way one thinks and behaves in solitude is what defines one's character. True measure of education is also in showing respect and politeness to others. Listening to a viewpoint or being tolerant of a different thought and opinion speak volumes of a person.

Forbearance and unfailing courtesy towards others,

irrespective of their culture, religion, language and behaviour, is a barometer for sound education. As a central force, education should reflect harmony and balance in thought, speech and action.

Change for the Better

Not that it hasn't been an ongoing process, but the past decade has seen a sea-change in Indian education policies. Various regulations and revised guidelines have come into being from time to time. Be it Teachers' Eligibility Test, change in assessment patterns, statutory reforms, learning management systems, rewriting and revision of textbooks or digitisation, gamification and virtual teachings, there have been many incorporations across states in India. The lines are getting blurred and free courses as well as downloadable sessions are getting increasingly available. Isn't education getting fancier with ERP solutions, virtual content, 3D imaging and 3D printing, AI laboratories and machine learning tools? We have a variety to spoil us and at the pace we are going, one can look forward to more digitisation in various aspects of education, further ensuring self-paced learning and individual attention to students for the best possible output. It is imperative now to move away from conservative subject rote learning to skill development and IT-enabled syllabus.

Of late, emphasis on rote learning has reduced, and so has marks-based assessment. Academics is no more about memorising and reproducing only to be able to score good marks or a rank. Those endless hours of memorising are a thing of yesterday and education focus has shifted to learning by doing, applied learning, project and activity-based learning, all of which enhance concept understanding in a way that can be applied to practical ground level situations.

Some innovations surprise and thrill, others make you want to do better. It is a good time to walk this phase.

The Journey Began Here

After stepping out of the gates of college, the first instinct is to begin work, to conceive projects and lead them to fruition. I must have been in my twenties when I realised that I am pretty individualistic in my style of work and that I have some innovative ideas along with an appetite for risk. Perhaps that was enough to get me started. Then again, there is no greater motivation than success. Success is what success does; looking back, I am glad my first venture was a success since that spurred me towards taking up more new initiatives. With every success, you build confidence and develop a knack for figuring out the pros and cons of undertaking newer ventures. I have been a true blue entrepreneur who has experienced enormous thrill in creating new projects and products along the way. Each of these projects was unique and put me on the path to self-assessment, which helped to exercise clarity in thinking and facilitated steps that were a mix of what-could-be and what-should-be-done.

School: Looking back, Focussing ahead

While growing up, one views education very differently, but as time passes, you realise how ideas and methodologies change. Back in school, I was always a good student, though not a topper. I remember there were many aspects of school and education that excited me; I was a singer, a dancer, a house captain, a sports captain. I was never a bookworm, nor was

I carried away by extracurricular activities. To me, overall development was of paramount importance, and somewhere along the way, when I began with the Kalorex schools, to achieve excellence in K-12 education, they were created with a clear vision of shaping glocal learners with commitment to provide a safe and stimulating environment, to prepare competent, compassionate and creative thinkers in this rapidly changing world.

Call of Technology

The last two-three decades have given us exposure to technological inventions that perhaps the world hadn't ever envisaged. Every day brings in newer innovations, lifestyle changes, product invasions, and humans while grappling with the switches, are stumbling, learning, incorporating and mastering them along the way. It is safe to say there are inventions by the hour. Tech-advancement has been the key driver in heralding change, especially in the education sector, in the past decade. Teachers have effectively been able to blend technology into a variety of subjects; they are growing as coaches, as content specialists.

Technology makes teaching and learning not only meaningful but a lot more fun. Students, on the other hand, are able to get together with their classmates through tech applications. School managers are able to monitor progress through various technological solutions, and parents are able to track performance as well as micro manage their child's growth.

Technology has been a boon for every stakeholder in education. With the number and variety of changes the past few years have seen, and the innovations the future will bring, the magnitude of change is likely to be greater still in this sector.

Incorporating Changes with Time

The pace at which everything around us is changing necessitates that we not only be alert but also well-researched about the changes and progress taking place in different spheres of education. What could help here is reading relevant articles, synopsis of books, industry reports and attending conferences, all of which are ways to keep abreast with happenings in the sector. These learnings then get translated into best practices and are carried forward in the teaching-learning process. Kalorex has been a forerunner in heralding change and it is this DNA that sets us apart. We strive to always be ahead of the curve.

Learning gives Clarity

Just as there are people who swear by formal education, there are also those who believe experience and learning on the job are as good as learning a subject formally. I would partially agree to this since experience is a great teacher. Learning on the job is a great way to acquire skill but concept clarity comes with learning and knowledge of the subject. Both aspects, learning as well as doing, make the whole. Traditionally, we first learn and then do, however, if someone wishes to do the reverse, which is first do and then learn, that would work too. The best mix, though, would be theory and practical side by side. There is a reason why subjects are streamlined, researched, studied and mastered and that is what education is all about. Being armed with learning is supporting oneself with skills that lend expertise.

Business Education

Nurturing a plan or a vision may be one aspect, but readiness to take risks around it to create and establish an enterprise or business proposition is something that requires more than just method. Entrepreneurship is a distinctive characteristic, an ability that requires a fair amount of research, reading and study of market trends; it requires a sense of persistence to get the task done, balance to believe in one's idea, ability to create a shared vision with the team, and the courage to stand alone when things don't turn out as planned. It needs attachment to the idea, yet a sense of detachment to be able to function as a professional.

I am not sure if all these traits can be taught through theory, but I would still advocate an entrepreneurship course, which will give people exposure to some of these requisites.

Boosting Entrepreneurship

There has been no dearth of opportunities for youngsters to venture into entrepreneurship. The government has come up with several campaigns like Skill India or Make in India to boost entrepreneurship in India. From fresh graduates to experienced professionals, with micro finance funding readily accessible, a lot many people are ready to dive into new businesses, to use their skills in establishing and running a company.

There are organisations that teach the art of writing project reports and provide mentoring to get started as an entrepreneur. There are university incubation centres that help project start-ups in the initial stages, and angel funding is also quite popular. The eco-system is all well laid out.

What an enterprise primarily needs is an entrepreneurial

mind-set, a trait that is very individual, it also requires drive and a well-chalked-out business plan to begin with.

Leading from the Front

There are achievements in one's journey that make everything worthwhile – not necessarily for the rewards and recognition, but the sense of gratification for having initiated and tried. Looking back, I'd say what paid off was my ability to see long term, to sustain a long vision. My ability to lead from the front under all circumstances has been a motivating factor to excel and keep at it; so has been the ability to retain professional people for over two decades. When Kalorex group celebrated its silver jubilee, it was a great feeling having people who have been loyal and have continued to serve the organisation since its inception. In walking, trudging and marching along, I have acquired the skill of being a compassionate yet strict leader with eyes focussed on results. And this perhaps has helped in achieving results, desirable and positive, relative and constant.

EDUCATION IS THE KEY FACTOR FOR PROGRESS IN SOCIETY, EVERYTHING THAT BUILDS AROUND YOU HAS ITS BASE IN IT. THIS PASSION FOR EDUCATION TURNING INTO PROFESSION ONLY ENRICHED THE PATH.

Ideas turn into purpose, and purpose wields passion. What makes them achievable is the will to deliberate upon and pursue them.

CHAPTER NINE

Plans, Projects And Perseverance

If not for thinking up unimaginable ideas and trying to give them some shape, life would indeed be dull, with little to stimulate, both, senses and surroundings. Of everything that living comprises, creating something has no equal. There is an enormous high in leading your thought to execution. And every hiccup or hindrance, that comes by, only teaches you to overcome and move ahead, focussed and determined. A lot of that which comes your way, or that which you desire and work to achieve, has its base in the strength of will. Some call it luck; some pure hard work, but it is worth reflecting how the foundation is simply your will. You 'will' things into your life – because you want them dear, or perhaps out of fear. Either way, they make it to you. That is perhaps why one is often told to pay close attention to thought and intent. For, it could turn real.

Talking Business

Many believe business runs in the family, in the blood. If the environment, when growing up, is conducive to business, it is quite natural to get a grip of the 'whats' and 'hows' of starting and regulating one. The thought process is developed based on all that is observed and passively learnt, which comes in handy when the time to dive into business arrives. While in many families, business acumen tends to get inherited through genes, there are several others, who have had achievers at home in subjects and fields incompatible with their line of business. Nonetheless, learning experiences of elders, whatever the field may be, are bound to teach and guide younger ones at home.

Venture Adventure

A lot depends on how we perceive our plan and its take-off. Is it a long-held desire you wish to accomplish or is something driving you on impulse? Whatever be it, it has to bring fulfilment.

I have always been a creator, and any creation I have considered or wished for, has fostered a sense of purpose and gratification. There are diverse skill sets you need when creating anything from scratch, and it involves immense risk-taking ability, besides novel ways of thinking and a lateral thought process. I have also realised that while there may be situations that call for taking immediate decisions, there are various other curves along the way. Small and large problems that crop up require to be resolved before you move forward. Failures cannot prevent you from moving ahead; you will not be successful in every plan but you have to learn to manoeuvre and find your way forward. There will be people you will learn from, and situations that will teach you. Dealing with little setbacks must not deviate you from your course. There will be times you will leap ahead, and times when you will crash. But you have to keep moving, with a firm resolve and a sharp focus.

Setting a Startup

Where do you really start? Formulate a plan, do some homework or be driven by conviction? It may be all of these, but what is primary is the conviction of purpose. There has to be certainty in what you wish to pursue and then you follow it up with sustained passion and plenty of homework. This would entail getting a grip of all the matters, starting from the business idea, its blueprint, executions and projections, to legal and statutory elements, financial aspects, technology, and taskforce potentiality and competence. There are innumerable things to streamline, and while the process is as interesting as it is challenging, it can get quite exasperating. But just as madness engulfs you, so does passion. And somehow, it is passion that helps you find a method in the madness. There are institutions and networking agencies that teach the art of entrepreneurship. There are government schemes for start-ups; it all starts with a bug of an innovative idea and the passion to create it. This is the starting and ending point for any entrepreneur.

Discipline First

There could be miles you wish to walk, and oceans you long to swim in, but these may remain merely thoughts and wishes in the absence of discipline. And for every target that is to be achieved, every plan that is to be put to action, there are discipline mantras you need to set for yourself.

I have followed a certain method to approach my aims. Three-year goals are broken down to yearly plans that need to be monitored each quarter. These goals are further broken down to weekly and daily tracking points. So, it is Plan, Act, Review, Re-plan and it continues thus. With no room for lethargy, no scope for mistakes or turning a blind eye to them, every step taken requires thorough planning, and nothing but discipline helps with leading plans to realisation.

Learning on the Job

No matter where, every person not only learns but also tends to get better when learning on the job. What it primarily provides is a sense of direction that motivates you to convert tasks at hand into assignments you own. However, for me, understanding business and taking risks, team-building and execution, turned out to be smoother since I was a student of Management. It helped me tremendously since theory is the pillar that sets the stage for practical action and implementation. Conceptual understanding, as I apprehend, is critical since it also helps in seeing the larger picture. If there is aptitude, going by the KSA theory (Knowledge, Skill, Abilities), anything can be accomplished.

So, what does business offer, and how does it prepare you? Most significantly, it teaches you to have 100 per cent accountability, besides having the ability to sort, organise and categorise information that enables decision-making. It supplements the ability to take hard decisions with a humane approach. It teaches you to be on the cutting edge of innovations, especially related to the objectives of the enterprise. And, this could be your key.

Meeting Success

No matter what line of business you choose, focus and clarity of direction is a prerequisite. Those running successful businesses tend to keep emotions at bay; their focus surrounds business growth where goals and targets are the key driving force. While still very young, I understood how necessary it is to be clear in the direction you want to head. If emotions slide in, your vision could blur. Thus, having that clarity allows you to make measured choices with less or nothing to pull you in opposite directions. And, success is a matter of time once you have set out with clear-cut goals.

Successful people normally tend to maintain good balance of work and leisure. For, often it is the leisure time that spurs creativity, much needed to smoothen out professional challenges. I also believe that successful people read and keep abreast of industry norms. They meditate, since that eases the process of looking inward, something that is often required when dealing with large groups and a variety of dispositions.

Woman on the Seat

Innumerable studies have been conducted to deduce whether or not women make better bosses than men and vice versa. Opinions have differed based on the essence of work, the cultural fabric of the region, and of course, the nature of women as collectively and largely understood by not just men but pretty much the entire world. I have built my understanding of it too. We're aware that every woman has an element of the man in her just as it is the other way round. Men are known to be more left brained (and thus more practical and reasoning) while women are primarily right brained (and therefore more emotional), but to have an androgynous mind ensures you have a harmonious mix of the two. However, being a woman boss prepared me to deal with men and, in the process, think in a more masculine fashion. Men tend to be logical and resort to application of reason more than women; they are also more objective and driven by data.

Tending to a Team

Be they male or female employees, teamwork is integral to the success of any project or business. A leader may have vision but without a sound team, the reach and process may not be conducive to the growth or success of the undertaking. If teamwork is thorough, the output is bound to be good. Individual minds, despite each excelling in its own sphere, may not be able to achieve a goal, but together as a team, it is likelier they meet their target. Teamwork is essential to ensure work does not suffer, people don't feel threatened or insecure and delays are avoided. Teamwork is also a great example of how things can be achieved if different people, with varied skills, get together to achieve something. Teams are also the reason for speed of action and smooth implementation of tasks.

A thing for Firsts

As an entrepreneur, I have constantly looked ahead, at opportunities that could turn fruitful, at projects that could drive me to excellence. There is plenty to learn from one's own undertakings and every experience is like an added feather in one's hat. And yet, there's something special about the first project. Like the first born child, the first project is always close to the heart, which in my case, has been Delhi Public School,

Bopal. It remains my most cherished venture and the reasons for it are innumerable too. Building this project gave me a 360-degree exposure, brick by brick. Be it civil construction that included architectural and structural engineering, understanding solar energy systems and installing panels, doing quality checks to customer orientation and statutory aspects, I detailed everything in the process of building my school. And this was learning of just one part. Regarding education and related introductions, demonstrating research abilities, considering pedagogical changes, legal framework and policy updates, there was something new waiting to be explored, understood and implemented, every single day.

The Visamo Kids project that deals with children from the underprivileged sections or the Prerna School for Dyslexics have been early initiatives that taught everything from researching and planning to execution. The various Calorx schools that offer unique teaching propositions have encouraged learning explorations with every new project. And, that is how learning is a constant. What each project offers, is the drive to create something new, of relevance, with responsibility.

Taking Risks

I am a hard-core entrepreneur at heart. Formulating projects gives me as much thrill as executing them does. Be it conceptualising or considering options, I enjoy the ambiguity that exists during the start-up stage, the varied aspects of learning that take place every time a new project kick-starts. The sense of the unknown that one is venturing into with a new mission is exciting to say the least. But there are risks involved, and as an entrepreneur, you have got to be able to stomach risks. There are some seen, some unseen and unknown variables at every step of the way. What can be tricky is that while one is working on moving ahead, some of what comes by can be beyond the imagination.

You have to stand prepared to face and deal with any challenge that comes up on your way forward. It is equally important to be able to patiently process it, understand and take your next steps. In all likelihood, most inputs will be useful but much of it can be given a pass. This is where using one's studied judgement, to be able to sieve from available information, comes in handy.

Reward of Creation

Every project involves not just hard work and consistent effort but also dreams that make the foundation stronger, dearer. I poured myself into creating beautiful schools where students besides learning, can grow and improve. I wanted the alumni to take pride in walking down the memory corridors and halls of fame there. I wanted the campuses to be a place where rich memories thrive, places that contribute to the making of young, individual lives.

Ever since the planning and setting up stages were active, I always maintained that when you start out, you drive the work. Soon enough the work consumes you, and you are driven by it. Opening and maintaining schools across several locations has been a challenge in itself.

The systems and processes that work beautifully in a single location, can create hindrances and difficulties when multiplied. And yet, running simultaneously several schools offered an opportunity to learn scalability of operations.

Driven by the passion of providing quality education, I find I am constantly challenging myself to stay ahead of the curve in every which way.

Takeaways Galore

Every project has its share of ups and downs, highs and lows, rewards and hiccups. But sailing through from misgivings to confidence, if there's something that is cherish-worthy, it is the self-dependence. My entrepreneurial journey has earned me respect and brought in a wealth of experiences. If I have learnt from challenging situations, I have also been gifted moments that raised my spirits. The overall gratification of bringing about transformational difference in the life of students is immense. I also believe that it has been spiritually uplifting to be instrumental in making young impressionable lives gain ground as they work with the sound backing of a fruitful education that opens doors for them to fresh avenues.

PERSEVERANCE WILL NEVER GO OUT OF FASHION. IT WILL DRIVE YOU, MAYBE EVEN DRAG YOU, BUT WILL NEVER EVER DISAPPOINT YOU.

It is not where she came from, it is what she is. Destiny kissed her, hard work stirred her up, she became a chariot of strength.

CHAPTER TEN

Women Of Substance

We are led to places we are meant to be. Somehow, I have always believed everything that happens in our life tutors us for something that is to come. In other words, everything that we live and confront eventually enables us to deal with what comes after it. Early childhood, therefore, has a major impact on the way we shape our lives, or rather, how life shapes us up. It is those initial experiences, be it expressions of love, the comfort of being understood, or taking up responsibilities diligently, that mould our present and design our tomorrow.

How we are nurtured is going to impact not only us but a lot of others we deal with. As a girl born to a loving mother and then mothering her due to her health concerns, my childhood, school and college days shaped a lot of what was to come in years that followed. Living in a hostel taught me emotional independence, and being in charge of the household provided me basic management skills while dealing with situations that necessitated decision-making. My self-confidence grew as I knew I had to be in charge – of myself and those that mattered.

My Circle of Women

I have grown to believe a mother is a great contributor in making the child unrestrained in spirit, with a keenly developed sense of individuality. For me, my mother's love, her trust, acceptance and unquestioned faith meant a feeling and sense of completion within myself.

My grand-aunt Didi has also been a strong role model and so also my mother-in-law who always believed that a woman must be an asset, never a liability. Be it Didi or my mother-in-law, both have been very traditional and conservative women yet pretty modern in their thinking and practical in their approach. One from Odisha and the other from Gujarat, these ladies have shown me that all women, across geographies and generations, need other women to empower them. Woman to woman empowerment is the strongest form of building self-reliance and confidence necessary to lead a fulfilling meaningful life. I feel glad these two strong women walked by my path.

My Force of Inspiration

We best understand the true essence of life from those who have inspired and moulded us in our early days. Those initial impressions form the essence of our thought process and belief systems only to stay on with us forever. The one person from whom I learnt the true meaning of living is my grandmother. Married off at only fourteen to a person thrice her age, she became a widow very young. She never went to school, and was illiterate, so to say. But in my life so far, I am yet to come across a person more educated and intelligent than her. The alacrity with which she handled revenue and legal matters, her clarity of thought and decisiveness in executing plans were remarkable. She was my first role-model and a really strong one at that. Another person I have subconsciously imbibed from, was the principal of my school.

I remember looking up to her for everything. The poise, the substance, the enigmatic presence she had and the manner in which she conducted herself, were all very appealing, especially her quiet assertiveness. The charisma, I still believe, was unmatched. As life graduated from being a carefree journey to one of weighing responsibilities and initiating concepts and projects, I came in touch with a host of people – professional associates, friends and colleagues – whom I observed and learnt from. Being an open and eager learner, I would always look at improving myself, one step at a time.

The Keen Incharge

Like they say, it all started quite young. I have received love in abundance and was a celebrated child. My independent streak was first sown when I was sent to a hostel as a five-year-old. Coupled with this, my mother's health issues resulted in me taking all the minor and major decisions at home. My father was away most of the time, so when I was home during vacations, I would take charge of running the household. Some decisions were related to medical matters, while others were basics like paying grocery bills, and even financial matters like allocating monthly funds for running the household.

I hadn't touched teenage, but I was handling money matters; it was a case of 'learning in progress' or I would say, 'learning on the job'. I distinctly remember a day where my school administrator spoke to me about delay in fee payment; until then, I did not even know there was a concept of paying fees in school! However, once I learnt the ropes, I undertook the reigns and responsibility of paying school fees on time, not just mine, but my younger brother's too, who studied in a different school.

Being a royal household, where the male child is the torchbearer and heir apparent, there were obvious discriminations between my younger brother and me, and I constantly challenged those. Only when I began to run the household and became responsible for most of the decision-making, did these discriminations stop and I was empowered through and through.

Women Empowerment

We live in a world that still debates whether women make good leaders or are men more effective in leadership positions. And this, after the world has seen women shine through not just in top leadership roles, but also in fields of science, research and technology. At the time when I started out, women-led organisations were actually few and far between. Things have undergone a change and yet, even today, there are less than 13 per cent women in board room positions and this is worldwide. It is no surprise then that the numbers were naturally skewed some twenty odd years ago.

Even if women did command a role or position, they had to work twice as hard to be taken seriously. I cannot say that did not happen to me. It did, and I saw myself having to prove my work and worth at every step. As a matter of tradition and thereby habit, men have always been taken more seriously at work. They receive recognition and credit for whatever they undertake, be it tasks, projects or leadership roles. But even today, women are paid less than their counterparts despite possessing the same skill sets in more than a few sectors.

To put it simply, all that women empowerment really means is freedom and equality – the freedom to express a thought, an idea, and be considered equal in thoughts, words and deeds. There should be some sense of equilibrium, the balance cannot be so skewed, women should not have to work harder just to prove themselves.

But one must accept that things have undergone a change in the last two decades, circumstances the world over have ensured that corporate women get their due. Over a period of time, as an entrepreneur, I have learnt how to always be taken seriously at work.

I was quite conscious of being a woman at the workplace when I had started out. Somewhere at the back of the mind was this feeling of having to work more to prove my worth. Gradually, as I began to handle more complex work, I figured out that gender really wasn't an 'issue', and that it did not matter.

What mattered was the ability to understand and be understanding, do hard work, be meritorious, take calculated risks, solve problems and be thorough in taking pertinent, timely decisions. Eventually, requisites for successful management were managerial skills and the ability to judge when to weigh options and when to step ahead.

When the Going Gets Tough...

Helming a large set-up can be exacting, something one realises only upon landing in that sphere. Managing a diverse set of people, with a broad range of mind-sets, can bring some challenging situations that you may not have envisaged at the outset.

I am not sure if it is related to my being a woman at the workplace or if it is my inherent characteristic, but I am very trusting. I believe that while one is trusting, excessive delegation could create troubling blind spots. Being a public figure and hence always in the lime light, where your life is under constant scrutiny, I have also faced some very challenging circumstances. Things are often magnified when they may be miniscule, and in some cases, even non-existent.

Facing Challenges

Of the many challenges I have faced as a woman, being able to walk into anyone's office at any time of the day would top the chart. As a woman, there are several protocols to be observed. I distinctly recall those many times when working long hours would be an issue. In fact, until I acquired a reasonable reputation of being a professional, male subordinates would constantly try to test my knowledge. Being a woman does any which way bring a set of challenges at the workspace, being an attractive one can surely bring in some extra rough weather. People tend to somehow not take you as seriously.

When I am a woman in a leadership position, are my goals any different than a man's in the same position? Perhaps men are more commercial and financially driven while women tend to nurture the welfare streak. The welfare and the creative are as important to me as are the financial aspects of the organisation.

Working Women, Working with Women

Being a woman, and a working woman, I have naturally come across both men and women co-workers, at all levels.

I have seen women in government sectors and higher offices, as social workers and organisation leaders; women are indeed a compassionate lot. In my area of work, I have enjoyed ideating, planning and executing various projects with women and often been pleasantly surprised by their drive and involvement. It is true women are natural multi-taskers, and play their part with sincerity. Their diligence and ability to be good managers make it a smooth sail when situations get challenging, when deadlines come calling. At the same time, there definitely are women one needs to watch out for, the kind who are consumed and driven by negativity. This is when one realises it takes all kinds to make the world. But that goes for both genders; men can be sugar-coated and dual-faced too. The sooner one understands and works around this with magnanimity, the easier the ride will be.

The Ambition Meter

Although it is tough to categorise all men and all women in sections, by and large women are less ambitious than men. It could be because they have their priority chart full. Often, competent women do not want to move out of their comfort zones to try something new. It wouldn't be a wrong assessment to say women enjoy a more laid-back life, have less fire to compete or win laurels, and the survival instinct is also lower. Women also take a break sometimes owing to lack of support or because they plan a hiatus from work, though once they resume, they do so with the same zeal and sincerity. I have especially noted that they indulge in less ambition-driven politics, and thus in fewer corporate games too. The ability to multi-task in women seems inherent, besides them possessing sensitivity, diligence and more regularity. There are some stereotypical qualities of women's group behaviours, which when controlled, can spike performance. So, while it is believed that women groups tend to gossip a lot, my experience is that gossip is not restricted to just women's groups; men gossip equally well.

If not a Woman...

I'd surely not desire to be a man. At the risk of sounding repetitive, I truly believe women are God's special creation and given a choice, I would love to be born a woman again. And then, there is the unparalleled gift and blessing of motherhood. Although I do feel I could have attained more speed being a man. That notwithstanding, I am not only content but feel privileged being a woman and nurture a strong creative bent which finds manifold expressions.

Having said that, had I been a man, I think I would have grown faster in my professional career, and would surely be less hesitant to stand for and get my job done aggressively. Aggression in a man is a celebrated trait but aggression in a woman is frowned upon. Who knows, I'd probably have travelled the world many times over and even been an adventure sportsperson. And yet, if I have made it today, it is due to my competencies, due to the ability to withstand cold winds. Blessings and providence apart, there is undeniably a lot of hard work.

Success Spelt My Way

Everyone builds upon an idea of how they would want their life to be. People have a very individualistic approach to measuring success and achievements. If material gains are a benchmark for some, top corporate seats could be a big draw for others. If a fleet of cars and fancy homes are what drive some, education in Ivy League colleges could be success for others. From the point of planning to pushing oneself in that direction, there is a supposed road to success that varies for all. The way I look at it, success is a sense of respect. To me, it is when people look up to you and realise you are made of solid mettle, that you cannot be broken. It is also when people who work for you not only trust your capabilities but also your value systems. It is in being confident of your decisions and being able to stand by them. Success is an attitude; it is the ability to walk alone.

> Sometimes you have to suffer in life not because you were bad but because you didn't realise where and when to stop being good.

How beautiful could it really be, this journey to motherhood. How less of it I actually knew, until I embarked on it.

CHAPTER ELEVEN

Motherhood

If ever there's something that leaves me at a loss of words, it is when asked to describe motherhood and all feelings associated with it. Motherhood cannot be described in a thousand words and yet 'complete' does some justice to it.

My mother loved me immensely and was such a fine example of selfless giving and nurturing, it was only natural I found that to be a way of life. Yet, when I had Advait, it was indescribable – this feeling of having a bundle with tiny hands and feet, a heart that beats and a mind that would, one day, engage – it was clearly the most beautiful feeling – enriching, elevating with a generous sprinkle of ecstatic charm. Romanticising how a mother is virtually omnipresent, how unbounded her love is, suddenly made sense. I looked forward to being a friend, philosopher, guide and above all, a security provider. Latching on to the idea of mothers being first role-models, I provided unconditional love and support to my son which gave me tremendous joy.

Coming Home

From gurgling and babbling to taking the first steps and then running, a child gifts you with rich experiences, and as days go by, you figure out the importance of being not just a bundle of energy but also a positive role model.

I was building Kalorex at that time and felt guilty many times over for having to leave my son behind and attend to work, but then, the times spent with him became even more special and cherished; I looked forward to coming home to him. At times I tried compensating by reaching home early. I trained the staff to ensure he was well cared for. I made it a point to always be around emotionally. His first online yahoo chat, I distinctly recall, was with me. Even as an infant he learnt to express himself through phone calls and I was able to share special moments with him. These are tiny landmarks which enrich your stock of delightful memories.

In the years that Advait was growing up, I hardly recall socialising. It was either him or work. Overnight travel without him was not an option. If anything, it was put off for some years. All said and done, it is difficult to strike a perfect balance. There were times I was more at home; then there were days I was more at work. Being my own boss did give me the advantage of flexible timings.

Another advantage of attaining motherhood was being able to appreciate other mothers and their problems. I was able to use this knowledge to their benefit. Kalorex, being a woman-driven and woman-dominant organisation, has very pro-women and friendly HR policies. Women do avail long leaves for children's final examinations, weddings or family events. Running institutions can teach you so much at various levels, the key spirit being understanding and compassion.

Love cannot Spoil

In those early years of parenting, the emotion of love for the child surpasses every other feeling. One is literally swept away by this overpowering emotion. This love finds a range of forms and expressions. Nothing seems enough and too much is never really too much.

But can immense love spoil? Perhaps turning a blind eye to mistakes and faults can, not providing timely guidance can, but love in itself can never spoil. As a parent, one has got to be intolerant of negative or brazen actions since it is known to lead to behavioural issues. Psychologists, too, have time and again recommended positive reinforcement as against punishment for personality development and smooth behavioural patterns set in growing-up stages.

Even if one is upset in dealing with an unfavourable situation or habit, the underlying feelings must invariably be those of love and affection. These are paramount in raising happy children. A child must feel safe even when being pulled up. Loving parents choose to respect and encourage, both verbally as well as through non-verbal tools, rather than blame or judge their offspring. Self-esteem, after all, only comes with a sense of self-worth built through positive affirmations, not by constant criticism.

While childhood ought to be a constant flow of endless outpourings of love, discipline cannot be a casual reference either. I am clear about the significance of disciplining yet being respectful of autonomy. Discipline is not a negative word, though is often misunderstood. Shouting and screaming or hitting children is not disciplining them; it is extremely important to be mindful of their emotional and psychological well-being. If they are scolded, blamed and talked down, the premise of discipline is surely being misused. I'd rather have it as a teaching moment where emphasis is on explaining or correcting negative or untoward behaviour. Children must know they cannot get away with everything. Distinguishing good from bad, positive from negative and favourable from unfavourable is necessary, but explaining these calmly and respectfully, is bound to yield positive results. Like I always believe: Discipline your child or somebody else will.

Innumerable opinions surround the theory of children getting spoilt and weak if pampered and indulged in. Can love ever weaken? On the contrary, it builds inner strength in the long run. Parents who mollycoddle, yet draw lines and build equal relationships with children, create strong bonds. If one slips into spoiling mode without being able to strike a balance of firmness, it could get troublesome. There are times parents hesitate to negotiate with children, reason or have frank conversations with them, and that is where issues arise.

With such views, those surrounding me have often wondered if I have overindulged my son. What I have done is tried to instil in him what I believe are fundamental learnings. Emotional intelligence is one thing I have concentrated on teaching him. In this era of machine learning and artificial intelligence, it is this quality that will steer him well. Another very important aspect I have drawn him to is to look within. No matter what the issue, the problem, the confusion, the answers are within us. All we need is to have trust, keep faith and connect with the inside.

Life Pointers

While there are no rule books for bringing up children, there are certain fundamental values that lie at the core. I have tried to walk that route with my son – compassion and kindness being as important as honesty in thought, speech and action. I taught him respectfulness for everyone – the old and young, rich and poor. Tolerance towards diverse cultures, thinking, and lifestyle is imperative and equally so is having patience to achieve results. I also concentrated on developing some skills like problem solving thus leading to course corrections and time management, which includes setting goals and preparing to-do lists.

You Get What You Give

How grossly unfair besides being incorrect it is for me to be relishing an ice-cream or sweet, but telling my child to stay away from it. Aren't we supposed to be positive role models? We have all seen how children learn by mirroring the actions of parents, more so in their early years. Being worthy of emulation to one's child is more desirable than being a strict disciplinarian. Whatever be the circumstances, I have almost always tried to explain the situation or the matter to my child, respected his feelings and treated him respectfully. I have not only been reciprocated with these but have abundantly got a lot more from him.

No matter how you bring up a child, he being rebellious or throwing tantrums is also a common part of growing up. But the way you handle these situations could determine the manner in which the child grows up to behave. Why not view rebellion as a healthy way of the child developing his personality, individuality and autonomy? I have tried to be understanding of it, and deal with it together with my child rather than brush it aside or be authoritative. Having said that, he has also been given sufficient occasions to take decisions, make choices, both of which build independence. For healthy autonomy to develop, a child's voice and opinion must be heard and discussed. When they get due respect as individuals, they understand what giving respect is like.

Tell or Talk

Two words very vital to the success of any form of communication, even one between the parent and child, are 'tell' and 'talk'. More often than not, I have sat down with my son and talked about important issues. He has always been a party to decisions that impact him. This doesn't mean there is no drawing the line; I am the mother and there are no negotiations on certain fronts, but there have been less occasions where decisions are declarations. One doesn't achieve much by telling but talking gets the communication going. I remember, no matter how young Advait was, I always talked to him and explained the reasons behind rules rather than asking him 'to do as told'. He has been encouraged to talk, express his feelings, and his opinions too have been heard and respected.

Learning from the Child

Unbelievable as it may sound, handling stress and anger is something I learnt from my child. Since he was like a sponge, soaking in and mimicking everything, I started correcting my way of handling stress. Every time I was anxious, it reflected in my child being unsure and troubled. It became essential for me to be able to manage stress and residual anger from work ensuring I don't carry and exhibit it at home. This largely gives the child a glimpse of how to behave when grown up. It teaches the child how to deal with stressful situations. This is in no way easy to achieve but being conscious and putting in an honest effort have helped achieve reasonable success.

Privilege, not Sacrifice

Does motherhood mean making sacrifices? How many times have we come across people either asking or suggesting this? Motherhood is a joyous experience with unbound joys and gratification. My son has helped me learn how to celebrate life. It is strange how motherhood is both, selfish and selfless. While the love and affection is without expectation and thus selfless; it tends to get selfish when you either want the child all to yourself or want to be at the top on their list, all the time. Children eventually grow up, the famous nest emptying takes place, which can be a very painful and tough experience to deal with. Can it be easy letting go of your child, away from your watchful loving eyes? To rear and bring up someone is a precious joy, a great fortune and a clear privilege.

Mother – First and Last Teacher

The world knows the mother as a child's first teacher. Nothing can shake this bond if it is strong. Next, teachers have a strong influence on children since they spend a lot of early developmental time with them. Without minimising the role of the teacher's influence in any way, my experience says no one can replace a mother. There have been parents who say that 'children only listen to the teacher'. Surely they listen and respect their teachers, but they also understand the mother's role. If nurtured well, a mother will always be the first teacher in a child's life.

Child Rights

Being around children has invariably made me view life from their perspective. It has made me understand how important it is for them to have views, wishes, concerns and rights. Child's Rights may have been in place in the Western world for a while now, but it is quickly gaining ground in India too. The origin of Child's Rights was to protect children, often small ones who hang around their working parents at work sites; this can be hazardous with severe repercussions of ill-health owing to low hygiene and safety conditions. Every child needs to feel safe, secure and be given the right to education. Each time we see a helpless child denied even the basics of food, shelter or education, don't we feel they have a right to it, at least as long as they are dependents?

Being Part of their Story

With families increasingly opting for nuclear set-ups, the large joint family system is almost non-existent, but spending time with grandparents, cousins, uncles and aunts is of paramount emotional value to young children. It takes a village to raise a child, we have all heard, haven't we? And how true it is! Children should grow up with lots of people around them so they can grow rapidly in every which way. Close gated communities offer a similar bonding. It helps the child emotionally, socially, mentally, psychologically and is responsible for creating their safe space, a place that provides them security and unbridled confidence. Interactions have known to open vistas for people across ages; imagine then what happens to a child when he/she has a wide range of people to meet with, learn from and turn to. Be a contributor to a child's life, sometimes just by listening and guiding, if not by doing or giving. You might be surprised how you could inspire a big move by a small act.

Motherhood teaches that it is in unconditional giving that the other learns. Unconditional love requires courage.

Nothing will ever come close to this phenomenon of being a parent. While everything may come and go, this remains a constant.

CHAPTER TWELVE

Parenting: The Mother Of All Joys

As a parent, you know your journey isn't just about correcting your children, telling them dos and don'ts, helping them in their homework or joining them at the playground. Parenting requires you to look into several aspects of their journey and these include emotional, social, psychological, mental and spiritual factors. It is all right to take interest in their Intelligence Quotient (IQ) but considering Emotional Quotient (EQ) is equally important, if not more.

Teaching children the art of dealing with emotions, not only their own, but also considering others', is key. Besides enabling them with empathy, it will foster understanding in their associations. It will also teach them to be mindful of the impact that interactions, associations, friendships and relationships can have on people. Likewise, their social skills will blossom if encouraged to meet and speak with people of varying age groups. Teaching children the art of having meaningful conversations, to trust in the goodness of people and be aware of all those they meet and interact with daily, would mean leading them to the right path.

Another predominant factor in the overall development of children is ensuring they have a sound and healthy psychological shield. Speak to them about not just their school and homework, or things they seek from you, but their likes and dislikes, their curiosities, their moments of thrill, and interests they wish to pursue.

It is extremely important to take time to understand what they do not like and the reason behind it. It is crucial that your children know they have your backing in case they face any problem and have trouble dealing with it. I pretty much believe that mental peace and calm are imperative for the sound growth of children.

The clearer their mind is, the better they will be at grasping things around them, be it study or play. There is no harm in letting your children take lead in decision-making since that will allow them to build clarity of thought.

The last, but most integral, is spiritual integration; sowing the seeds of faith and worship in children will allow them to seek spiritual support with the faith that they will receive grace. As they move ahead in life's journey, they will know, understand and be aware of things that happen with them and around them.

Reliance on the Supreme can pull you through the darkest of phases; as a parent, it is you who can help them build that faith.

Bundle of Contradictions

Parenting seems enjoyable and easy, difficult and demanding, and everything else in between. Being a parent provides the greatest security but it also snowballs a host of insecurities. While there is no greater feeling than knowing you have someone who is your own to go through life with, living and loving its journey, there are also several moments when you are in precarious situations, when you either sense trouble or uncertainty with regards to your children.

As I have said before, contradictory as it may be, parenting is both, selfless and selfish. There is nothing you weigh before you do anything for your children, you want to give them most selflessly the very best, without expecting anything whatsoever in return. Having said that, you are also selfish – you want them to believe and feel that you are the best parent; you want them to listen to you and fulfil your wishes; you want to be their undivided world, just like they are yours. For me, motherhood has been about absolute nurturing and complete disciplining as well. It is a role for all seasons, summer and winter days, autumn and spring time too. Motherhood is eternal and spiritual.

The 5F Mandate

A prominent objective of parenting could be introducing to your children what I believe is the '5F Mandate: Faith, Family, Friends, Finance, Fitness'. There is nothing more powerful than hope, belief and faith, nothing more important than the comfort and love of the family, no joy akin to the company of good friends, perhaps no better knowledge to steer you through life's practicality than a good understanding of finance, and clearly nothing that can give you the bonus of good health, vitality and exuberance than keeping up with the discipline of staying fit.

Striking a Balance

No matter what aspect of life you deal with, you realise nothing is possible unless there is a good balance in your approach and expectation. Parenting adopts the same route as well. There is always a tussle between how much to expect from the kid, how much is too much and how little is too little. There are also questions you don't quite have a ready answer to. Is being too tough detrimental or is being too lenient a recipe for disaster; how much can you let go and how insistent must you be; how much to refrain and how much to give in; how strict must the rules be, and where all can they have a free hand? Overarching a variety of factors, I believe undiluted love is the greatest gift of parenting.

Simply being intuitive doesn't quite cut it; I have read several books while I was actively engaged in parenting. Beyond books is the world of observation, of people and circumstances, that helps in understanding, engaging and taking measures. To this day, my son Advait and I have discussions on a variety of subjects, concerns and issues. Considering he is a full grown individual now, I simply try to watch out for his emotional wellbeing. One assumes and prays the offspring is old enough to handle and manage other things.

Gift of Reciprocation

In a world that calculates every step and decision, parenting gifts you the joy of understanding and enjoying the act and feeling of reciprocation. There are several parents who hold themselves back fearing rejection from children, if not at that instant, then perhaps at a later age and stage. The point is in doing whatever it be for them, wholeheartedly. It is in being there for your children completely, in responding to them with love, listening to them intently and showering them with assurances that promise them security.

When my son was still a little boy, I would initiate actions that would enable him to reciprocate. Citing one, I recall how each time I left him home and went outstation for work, I would try and get back the same day even if it was very late, and go to see and hug him on reaching home. I saw this reciprocation when he grew up; no matter how late he got home, he would invariably come to my room and let me know he was back. He has also seemingly noted my prioritised interest in journal-writing, and every time I went through tough situations, he would remind and check whether or not I was writing one.

While children learn from and emulate us considerably, it is little rewards that are ours to keep, like his recently telling me, 'You are my strength and I am yours'. Love begets love, there's little else that can say so much in limited words.

Valuing the Invaluable

Often, while enjoying what we are blessed with, we tend to unknowingly ignore the plight of others, we take for granted that which comes to us easy. Gratefulness and compassion are both fundamental components in living a meaningful existence, for it is in being grateful and compassionate that our true selves are revealed. When I was a young mother, I was also building Delhi Public School, and I recall how Advait enjoyed playing in the sand along with children of labourers. He wanted servants' kids to sleep in the same bed as his and was very keen on making them comfortable. Today, he is grateful to the househelps for all they do for him, and shares a unique equation with them. Perhaps that is why the home staff, including the security guard and the driver, buy balloons and celebrate when they go to receive him at the airport each time he visits home from college abroad. It is in these little acts that I saw how kindness and affection with anyone can be reciprocal.

I like to listen to my son and understand how his thoughts and aspirations have evolved over time... from wanting to help the needy and looking after autistic children in school, he now dreams and aspires to help poor kids and make India poverty-free. As a parent I feel proud to know his thoughts and to understand how well grounded he is.

Adopting a Parenting Style

I have been a very strict professional and could have ended up being either a tiger mom or a helicopter parent but thankfully I did not take that route. To me, shaping Advait to be an individual with a voice and view was paramount, and hence I was more a permissive mom during his younger days, and more of an authoritative one when he grew up.

Pratul has been an exceptional father, someone easy to approach, easy to talk to; he has also been a friend standing shoulder to shoulder with him. Together, they play board games, do outdoor trekking and even chat with each other for hours. Having said that, demanding academic and financial discipline from our son isn't something Pratul overlooked or gave less importance to. He believes parenting to be a fine mix of fun and togetherness, at the same time seeking the best efforts from your child in his journey towards a happy and fulfilling life.

Tantrum, Discipline, Negotiation

Temper tantrums is one thing every parent on the planet has faced. There are situations involving extreme highs and lows when parents find it tough dealing with kids' tantrums, but the simplest and most effective way to get them to be reasonable is talking to them. Besides patiently listening to them, offering them logical explanations to the many questions simmering in their heads is the only way to move forward. Disciplining kids is necessary and that does not have to mean scolding or shouting at them. It is also not about punishing or reprimanding your children. It is, instead, instilling desirable habits in them by being reasonable and logical, by lovingly and patiently putting across your point of concern.

Do not hesitate to negotiate with children when necessary, where it is no longer about what you want or what they want. Let it be a common projection of 'we' in place of 'you' or 'me'. Opt to take a route that you both think is good instead of having your way or letting them have theirs. Bridging your opinions will allow you room for reasoning and that could instil confidence in them.

Turning Rivalry to Revelry

How well your children fare with others and how well they get along with their siblings will have a lot to do with how you foster love and understanding among them. Your approach and behaviour with each one, especially in front of the other, is integral to how they will behave when they are with each other. Without taking sides, be appreciative of each, but choose to recognise and hone the positive quality of each child. This will encourage them to acknowledge and admire their sibling without feeling threatened. They will be able to celebrate their uniqueness which will boost not only their confidence but their self-esteem considerably.

As a parent, it is very easy and tempting to compare them and talk highly about the positive traits of the other. While there is no harm in doing that, identifying their uniqueness is equally imperative. For, ultimately you want them to get along with each other besides having individual personalities. Enjoy your time with your children, but also ensure you have engaging conversations with them, even if it is only for a few minutes.

It may matter little how long you spoke but it will significantly impact what the subject and quality of talk is. When each child feels loved, desired and cared for, they will have a harmonious bond. Another key factor in ensuring a great rapport between siblings is to never leave issues and conflicts unresolved. As parents, approaching the issue with reason and understanding will take care of frustration and erratic anger eruptions. Nothing will fuel the sense of security in children than generous doses of love and affection.

Gift Check

You want to shower gifts upon your children each time they do well in exams, on birthdays, during vacations and every time you return from work tours. It is only natural for you as a parent to want to gift them something that is both, desirable and innovative. But do you feel your frequency of gifting is increasing not just because there are too many toys and gadgets available, but because you are subconsciously covering up for the lack of time you are able to give them due to work and other commitments?

Often parents who are guilt-driven end up expressing love by surprising their children ever so often with gifts, believing that may compensate or cover up for the lack of time they spend with them. Today gifts are no more restricted to books, stationery and board games. A wide range of electronic games and gadgets have invaded the market and children are too aware of all the latest ones available. While it is natural for you to want to expose them to new games, it may help to be mindful of what you give them and understand whether or not you are gifting them more than is required.

Parenting in present times is perhaps more engaging and interactive than it used to be a couple of decades ago. However, often the gifts we end up buying are not something they require but tend to be things bought by us to assuage out guilt for not spending adequate time with them. This guilt of leading a busy office life or going on frequent office trips pushes parents to buy more and more expensive gifts as a means to make amends. In the process, unfortunately, children lose the value of carefully selected gifts and develop the habit of discarding the old ones as soon as new ones arrive. In the long run, this could be damaging since it may not allow children to cherish what they receive.

With plenty of virtual stores offering variety, promotional offers and heavy discounts on a wide range of branded products, children get drawn into the fancy world. But that is precisely where parents need to get alert. It would help to speak to children and explain how there is no need to hoard gadgets or fancy brands as these form part of a fashion cycle that changes faster than seasons.

A MEANINGFUL CONVERSATION FOLLOWED BY A MUSIC SESSION WITH LOVED ONES COULD BE MORE VALUABLE THAN GIFTS BOUGHT WITH MONEY.

It isn't tough to individuate the relationships that comfort. Every bond spills magic from time to time.

CHAPTER THIRTEEN

Connected By Choice

We are all born connected, either by blood or by chance. The latter translates through destiny or desire, depending on personal belief, understanding and outlook. But the little voice within tells you who is yours and who is not, what is right and what is not. Life experiences, lessons and journeys are enhanced owing to the people around us – family that stands rock-solid, friends who encourage, associates who inspire, loving bonds that shape our tomorrows. There is no dearth to learning, and much of what we determine and discover is responsible for moulding our thought process and subsequent moves.

And then, there are deep bonds with deeper impacts. They are life-altering and, interestingly, life restoring too. Some get classified into categories, while some mature and move away from the confines of merely being a man-woman relationship. Those are the ones that never fade, the kinds that keep the shine on. While care for the other is naturally ongoing, boundaries of time and period cease to exist. Romance and marriage are milestones of life, just like crawling, walking, running and speaking are milestones for children. It is when you move beyond these milestones that possibilities for richer relationships embrace you.

Sound Relationships are Rewarding

What is human life without relationships? Bonds forged along the way are what keep alive the spark in life. Some call them connections of the heart, others believe they are what keep the boat afloat. Music, dance, travel and outdoor adventure are other joys that double when you have a companion to share common interests with.

And then, there are other relationships which are equally important – as mother, sister, sister-in-law, daughter, daughter-in-law, wife, friend and boss. Each one comes with its dynamics, challenges and substance. Nurturing and growing each of these relationships is important. Some may come easier than others, but they all have their own place, and their own unique essence. What perhaps is important is being mindful of the other, keeping the other before you. Understanding their interests and requirements gives comfort, which is what a relationship truly strives for. Sounds easier said than done? It might, but genuine care for the other is sure to reward you with love that lifts, joys that are unmatched.

Whiff of Romance

Early impressions and associated memories rarely die down. Glorified as they may be, they make home in the deep recesses only to spring up as thoughts once in a while. I have always had a fancy for uncommon marriages, when people who don't speak the same language marry, when people from diametrically different cultures come together, when dissimilar people end up spending lives together. It is intriguing for me because that proves the maxim 'Love is blind'. It shows there is no reasoning to matters of the heart, that logic fails where love makes home. I have done something similar, broken the shackles of custom and married someone of my choice.

Of Mush and Crush

As much as we enjoy and cherish our present, we all enjoy walking back to our yesterdays – days of carefree joys, innocent infatuations, and early crushes. For me, my earliest crush was Rishi Kapoor. I remember wearing bell-bottoms like him; I would also sing and dance like him. Films tend to impact our formative years in a way, influencing our fashion, lifestyle and our perception of romance, even though their portrayal may be glorified and unrealistic.

Since my early years were filled with responsibilities, I had little time to digress from my chosen path, which was my career. Bonds of love, as a matter-of-fact, happened along the way, friends came and stayed on, and romancing life seemed just as tempting.

The Sway of Influence

Relationships and friendships have always been about connecting on a level that is beyond reason or season. While parameters of friendship are difficult to define, a lot has changed in the last two decades or so when it comes to things friends do together. Today sitcoms and films dictate a lot of what kids do in their time together; there is no denying that visual media influences in ways that cannot quite be defined or classified.

Today it is not just films and television, there is the internet too that deeply impacts children. Everything is situational so you cannot categorise anything as entirely good or bad. *Friends*, a western tele-series with western values, is popular with children in our country too, and most surely their value system gets impacted watching it. Balancing what they think is real with the ground realities within the Indian cultural context is a tough struggle. The same applies to love, romance and ideas of marriage as well.

Emotional and Sensitive – To Be or Not To Be

There are far too many views about being emotional and sensitive, various schools of thought that point out the benefits and drawbacks of being sensitive and emotional as a person. I, for one, see it as a strength to be both. One is able to connect with another person instantly and it can be the source of lasting relationships. Being emotional can sometimes be construed as a weakness, but that would be in case a person gets overtly carried away by emotions. Where decisions are taken purely on emotions without reliance on data analysis or facts, it could prove to be a hindrance, especially at work place. Optimisation could be the key to more or less everything, including emotions.

Self-worth comes from the Self

Love and relationships can make one feel secure and wanted. Relationships, perhaps like dark chocolate, release serotonin and another feel-good hormone, dopamine; the feeling of self-worth is enhanced and there is possibly nothing that feels greater than that. However, building relationships is not the only way one derives self-worth, although relationships do play a significant role in society since humans are social animals. While I do appreciate the couple goals (often proudly announced on social media) of some of my acquaintances, life to me is an individual journey. Every relationship plays its designated role at the time it is meant to, but eventually we are eternal travellers in this journey of life, each of us undertaking an odyssey of our own.

Siblings are Forever

The deep joy of having siblings is knowing that while the world can nail you down, there are those who will always stand beside you to ensure you sail. That is the bond and love siblings share. My brother died young and thus my memories with him are full of nostalgia. My major fights were also always with him; we have actually had sword fights with curtain rods.

I also recollect some fun episodes, laced with moments that seemed extremely funny then, but are cherished memories now. Every family has its set of customs and practices; in our home, the elders in the palace would wake up my brother, make him walk to my room with closed eyes, and then make him look at me first thing in the morning since it was considered auspicious. My brother would hate that; he would ask me how that would help him get good grades in school! Back then, I too never quite understood the significance of everyone waking up to come and see me first thing in the morning. But all said and done, it was sheer delight to see how annoying the entire experience was for my brother. In hindsight, who knew what life held for each of us. But the relationship between siblings is special. It strengthens and maintains you.

For a major part of my initial years, I had my sister to fall back on for a lot of growing-up issues. She is barely a year older than me, and looking back I am sure it may have been quite a load on her.

But all said and done, I have mostly relied on myself, on my inner voice. My gut feelings, my instincts and my faith in the larger good are what have kept me going, irrespective of anything. It is this absolute and continuous dependence on the inner self that has sharpened my ability to look inward and be self-reliant.

The Marriage Course

Love definitely, but I think common value systems solidify a relationship that is sealed by marriage. In India, arranged marriages tend to work; it could be possible that synergy of family backgrounds and common values take precedence. Though marriage can be quite like '*Dilli ka laddoo – jo khaaye woh pachhtaye, jo na khaaye woh bhi pachhtaye*' (Marriage is like the special Delhi sweet – you regret if you have it, and regret even if you don't). Until one is married, there is a tremendous aspiration associated to marriage; however, once married, the biggest jokes going around are on spouses!

But jest and quips aside, marriage provides the greatest opportunities to learn, grow and stand by each other. Marriage comes with a basketful of responsibilities, several twists and turns too, but once you are in it, there is a sense of duty that needs to be fulfilled as well. It is about giving your word and living up to it.

The CEO Couple

There is plenty in the world that can bring two people together. For Pratul and me, a common interest in Management led us to a common path. It is true we first met at the Indian Institute of Management in Ahmedabad, but our interest in Management as a subject of study has driven us a great deal.

It goes beyond just books and methodologies. We are both quite distinct as leaders, be it in our approach to work or situations. Pratul's engineering background tends to make him data driven, with greater focus on details. I, on the other hand, am more strategic and extremely decentralised in my approach.

Being CEOs in our respective careers has helped understand each other's time, travel and work commitments. Mutual respect, therefore, comes easy.

Management is a key element of life, something that teaches us balance and the ability to accept everything for what it is. Management teaches rationale, reasoning, and helps create a long-term vision.

We also have individualistic personalities; where Pratul is largely an introvert, who opens up only to a few close set of people, I am gregarious and pretty much an extrovert despite being an extremely private person with only a handful of confidantes.

We are also from the two opposite coasts of India, me from the East coast and Pratul from the West; it wasn't just a blend of language and customs, but a blend in almost every aspect of life ranging from food and clothes to environment and culture. Leading our teams individually has contributed to much of our work life being focussed, enterprising and dedicated to clearing paths and planning ahead.

A Child of One's Own

True love is never quite felt, or understood, until you have a child of your own. To me, the bond between a parent and child is of utmost significance. Being a parent takes the art of giving to heights one cannot even begin to comprehend. The meaning of unconditional assumes reality. It is this unique bond that sets the foundation of the child's character and personality. This relationship provides the highest degree of gratification. The parent-child relationship is not without challenges, but it is also worth living it, every minute of it.

For me the biggest joy has been motherhood. It may sound repetitive or clichéd, but there is no greater gift on earth than becoming a mother. My maternal sense is very enhanced, and that is why I enjoy my work with children so immensely, so passionately. I relate to children more than I relate to adults and have a natural bent towards an innate understanding of young children, their emotions and thought processes.

Love Makes, not Breaks

As extreme as love can be, pain or heartbreak too are viewed as extreme emotions, the kinds that make or break. There can be many learnings from broken or ended relationships but whether these learnings cause significant changes or not would depend largely on the person going through it. Some people take their lessons from every situation, good or bad, and move forward. And then, there are those who choose to ignore or overlook life's lessons. Ironically, life has a way of repeating the same lessons to us, until they are understood and learnt.

Heartbreaks, however, are not necessary for individual growth, as has been glamorously portrayed off and on. Had it been so, the best poets and singers of the world would not be able to emote as much, until they had had sufficient experience in heartbreaks. We have all seen teenagers sing with intensity and passion; it is unlikely that they have experienced pain at that age, and yet they do it beautifully.

While I was growing up, I associated pain with intensity. It is a general myth that more pain equals to more intensity. I would like to believe exactly the opposite. Pain can be a limiting negative emotion. I am not referring to the 'no pain no gain' theory; that is a phrase fit for use in the gym and fitness world to refer to sweet pain when one does muscle training sufficiently and they are left sore due to the release of lactic acid. Any negative pain associated with relationships is something to watch out for. If it is harming, you need to sit up and check. Love and relationships are meant to be celebrated. Since love is a positive emotion, that is the way it has to be conducted.

Work Camaraderie

There are so many things you learn once you begin your professional journey. It isn't one or two people you learn from, but a host of them who you work with along the way. They make a difference in your life, help develop perspective and contribute to your growth. I have learnt so many different things from different people. My first boss taught me decentralisation, from the second one I learnt detailing. My subordinates taught me to inspire and not be authoritative, while my peers taught me to listen. Students have continuously challenged us and in the process helped in problem-solving, whereas parents have taught us to be firm yet polite and to listen with compassion.

Our Kalorex Service Promise aptly reads: 'To hold an umbrella over their head while it rains'. Everything, indeed, has been a 360-degree growth.

Love, Power, Money

Each of these is assumed to be driving the world. But let's begin with love, which is infinite. Love is the real essence of mankind, and limiting it to genders and two-way relationships, means narrowing down the meaning of love. Love is the lubricant that makes everything move, animate and inanimate. We all function better when we are loved, we all are driven when we love.

Power and money, on the other hand, are narrowing. Tangible goals often circle around money and power, but that is so restricting. You can have both but without joy and love, these may seem empty and meaningless.

Life must be limitless, and without love, it can never be so.

SELF-WORTH AND CONFIDENCE ARE YOUR OWN PERSONAL ARMOURS. PRAYERS AND MEDITATION MAKE THE IMPOSSIBLE POSSIBLE, THE UNBEARABLE MORE ACCEPTABLE.

Recreation often leads to newer ideas, renewed energy. A song here and a dance there, it has made all the difference.

CHAPTER FOURTEEN

Life Beyond Work

I believe I have very consciously indulged in a few whims, pursued some childhood interests, and being artistically occupied tops the list. A passionate inclination towards performing arts, particularly music and dance, has most surely been one of the strongest rejuvenators in an otherwise busy life.

Memories from school come flooding – the drawing and painting classes, the music sessions, the essaying of a random role in some dramatic presentation. Somewhere, each one of us has these early school memories, a platform that harbours our likes and desires. And along the many twists and turns that life springs forth, it is these very interests that make the ride worthwhile. Being neck-deep in work does not seem too bad when you know you have some music to soothe you, some dance steps to liven you up at the end of a busy day. Such interests have been known to keep stress at bay, often cushioning the mind to believe there's more to life than just existing from one file to another.

Singing and dancing have always been important to me. Had life not thrown so many challenges my way, I sure would have chosen a creative career. In fact, day-to-day challenges made creative pursuits seem like a luxury at times. And yet, I am glad I got to enjoy a close proximity with multiple creative recreations.

All Work, Some Play

It is largely believed, especially in India, that if you have a busy work life, interests would decidedly take a backseat. Thankfully, that hasn't always been the case with me. I have plenty of right-brain interests, not just now, but ever since I can remember. I believe that work life would have been extremely mundane had I not got the opportunity and chance to explore my creative side. It is also this immersion in creative activities that allows me to go on, and keep exploring.

Creativity keeps the buoyancy and zest for life alive. It could be breaking into a dance step or trying out a new song, perhaps enjoying an evening of poetic exchanges or simply dancing the blues away. Whatever be it, the lighter side is what adds spice to a routine life, and provides the much required lift. Of course, there have to be limits set to everything when you lead an engaging and elaborate life. In mine, I'd give 65 per cent weightage to my professional life since it is quite demanding and 35 per cent to pursuing finer interests. But like with everything, there's some planning that goes in and thus weekends are reserved for creative exploration. Late nights and early mornings are my usual getaways to greet my inner core. They are for nursing little wishes and joys that spring within, be it a hobby break, catching up on reading a long-pending book or simply scribbling in my personal journal.

Lights, Camera, Action

A major part of my life has been spent in public domain which sort of sanctioned me a camera-friendly life. Several opportunities came for modelling, acting and fashion showcasing, but somehow I never gave it serious thought. The root for this could lie in the fact that in my growing-up years I was busy trying to get a hold of life for myself and the family. Also, coming from a conservative background, stepping out to build an enterprise was big enough a challenge; embracing the glamour world or even giving it a try was beyond the scope of even imagination! My family would not have accepted it and hence I never watered those thoughts.

As a teenager though, modelling wasn't a choice, and with acting too, it's just been a role here and a role there, off and on. But it was fashion that wooed me which is when I decided to do a few cat-walk sessions for Visamo Kids Foundation, Save the Girl Child, and Women Empowerment among others. I have also developed an individual fashion style over the years; it isn't about clothing alone; fashion is a mind-set. I follow my own comfort and interest and wouldn't wear something just because it is trending. Having an individualistic mind-set makes it easy to distinguish and incorporate preferences.

Like many of us have, I did some theatre acting and dance drama while growing up. There is a charm to acting since it gives you an opportunity to escape to another world, live another life. Getting into a character, different from your own, willingly transports you to an imaginary could-be world. It lets you think how to live that role, that life. By being another character, you are able to shape your personality too. It triggers the imagination and motivates you to think of variations you can put forth, although I must add, it is not easy to act. It may seem easy at the outset, but as they say, a camera never lies. Even the slightest over-acting or loosening up reveals the inability to get into the skin of the character. And if your homework before the act isn't up to the mark, it won't appear genuine and 'real'. It is interesting how something that actually seems easy requires minute observation; what you want to show, has to be mentally and emotionally processed first, before you relay it to others.

Sing and Dance your way Through

Singing and dancing is so much a part of my life, I find it difficult to believe these don't figure somewhere on top in every person's list of must-dos or favourite pastimes. For me, songs playing on the radio, some music when lounging around with a book, high-energy songs while travelling by road, are part of my existence. I believe my creative pursuits, especially singing and dancing, have helped me bounce back from edgy and challenging situations. They have also helped me fight monotony and stagnation. Every time I pursue my key interests, I feel recharged and am able to attend to the same task many times over, to the point of excellence. Folk dance is my piece de resistance. I learnt Odissi while growing up but got passionate about garba once I came to Gujarat and learnt this very popular dance form.

The movement in dance, the rhythm in music, both teach the beauty of detail; they show you there's no short-cut. And once you pay attention to details, the performance escalates. The same could be applied to work as well. Staying focussed and attending to details can smoothen work without making the process a burden. For, haven't we heard, devil is in the details!

I have often felt that work becomes easier and more productive only when there is something to balance out the pressure, the stress, the monotony that sets in. Interests and creative pursuits harmonise our lives, which are otherwise full of twists and turns. There are changes, there are setbacks, and then there is the continuous progression of days that pack in all these. Being deeply rooted to some creative form helps latch on to a sense of peace and calm. Also, making some time for indulging in creativity keeps you from experiencing restlessness. It eases the mind to know there is something it can turn to, despite circumstances that may seem overwhelming. Viewing a situation calmly, more often than not, sets forth the right path.

Music to My Ears

There is nothing like music to fill silences at times when you want to be alone, or at times when you end up in solitude due to circumstances. At such times, for most people, across continents, it is music that rejuvenates the spark much required to get going from day to day. One has heard different kinds of music – classics, instrumental, country, meditative – playing at restaurants, art galleries, public gatherings, health clinics, which goes to prove that music is prerequisite to a happy existence. Music is called the language of the soul because it can be understood by everyone. Where words fail, music expresses; it also mirrors the innermost feelings. I have noticed how the mood changes, sometimes based on a tune, otherwise owing to an emotive line from a soulful song. Music has soothed and healed souls, it has reignited and restored the spark that keeps life from fragmenting into nothingness. Physical activities like exercising and jogging, yoga or even long walks become even more enjoyable when coupled with music. *Raag Yaman* is one of my favourite ragas, another one that comes close is *Raag Bhairav*.

Mediate, Meditate

Amidst the humdrum of daily life, there are a few things that give you peace, allow you to unwind. Meditation for me is the channel that connects me to my inner self, a place I get all my answers from. I do it often, I enjoy sitting still and quiet with only soothing meditation music for company. I have found my doubts cleared in silent surroundings, with growing awareness of every moment, gently sailing in to the deep recesses. I totally believe that just as questions spring within us, so do responses and answers.

Online is in Vogue

Innovations in science and technology have new things to offer every single day, year after year. The virtual online world comes with offerings galore but the temptations also are too many. From films and fashion to music and dance, there's nothing quite out there that does not mix learning with competition and viewing with acquisition. The internet makes it easy to follow anything – from a deep-rooted desire of years to something you heard of and saw only a few days ago.

There's a good that comes from everything even remotely

bad or unpleasant. The lockdown, owing to the Covid-19 pandemic that had the world in its grip from day one, opened creative doors through outlets available online alongside mandatory learning. I have been in Gujarat for several years without indulging in a favourite pastime of mine which was singing. I was lucky to reconnect to it during this very period. The lockdown has its own stories for each of us, but there's no denying that the online world was not only an escape but a companion that helped us stay sane, and more importantly, in touch with the world around. At our organisations, for instance, every teacher had to pursue a course in online teaching to ensure better grip over tools and teaching methodology.

A Year to Remember

The year 2020 was like none other; while it sprung surprises for many, it turned the entire world topsy-turvy. Many lost near and dear ones, many more lost livelihoods. We came to witness a lifestyle we never ever imagined. The whole world was shaken.

Although maintaining a balance in these trying times wasn't quite easy, the lockdown saw a surge in creative diversions. I got the opportunity to dedicate an hour to singing every single day. I have been a reasonably good singer, though many who know me are unaware of it, perhaps because my passion for dance invariably takes over.

It has also been commendable how the world was adapting to changes and moving forward. Professionally, this hiatus helped us think over and create an online portal for learning and education, something that lent meaning to this unexpected change across the world.

The Voice Within

For as long as I remember, I have always been an intuitive person. There has been a guiding light within, showing me the direction I must take, and I have been very mindful of the signals that came forth. I am compassionate but driven by results. It is these attributes that have shaped me to be a leader who is not afraid of speaking her mind and demanding results. A leader who cares in the real sense; I lead from the front and handle success and failure with a humanistic approach. And, amidst all this, I sing and dance to keep life going.

Happy 'diversions' on your road to success lead to enhanced productivity.

A bit of me set out on journey, but a lot of me meandered back. It was time to live more stories, and I found wings.

CHAPTER FIFTEEN

Forever A Traveller

At times it feels as if many short films dwell in me, running through the deep recesses of my mind, one after another. They are stories of joy and courage, wonder and enchantment. I have been spectator to some, others I have lived. But each one has stirred my senses and satiated my soul. Travel has, irrevocably, gifted me multiple lives, all in one lifetime.

Besides endorsing fun-filled experiences, travel is a great leveller, and above all, a sublime healer. Encouraging the self to move beyond familiar boundaries to station at a new place, try an offbeat cuisine, revel in another culture, and live through different parts of the world is serendipitous to say the least. Travel provides opportunities for learning valuable life lessons, which can be very rewarding. Travel opens up the mind to new cultures and customs, teaches us to embrace tolerance to different ethnic groups, different mind-sets, encourages to experiment with new cuisines, basically to live life to the fullest.

Seeking Travel

If anything, I believe people are meant to travel… to explore new places and get a glimpse of life in a world beyond their own. Stepping into a new space is therapeutic to some, joy-inducing to others. It broadens horizons and affectionately nudges you to walk through a different world, to gather pieces of your soul waiting to be one again.

Travelling in our family has been an annual affair. Summer was typically abroad and Diwali time meant travel within India. As long as it was packing bags and setting out, the destination never mattered – be it adventure or spiritual travel, plain sightseeing or luxury getaways. I can wander about aimlessly, pounding pebbled streets, looking for sunset hues, or just stop and enjoy a hot cup of freshly brewed coffee. Words can't express the charm of exploring quaint places on foot. Then, there have been times I have simply allowed myself to soak in the luxury of some timeless hotel, or spaciously spread out theme resort. I have trekked, biked and sailed. I could never ever imagine a life without travel.

Unequalled Equalizer

Having travelled across the country and to far corners of the world, I can call myself an international citizen now. Each time I travel, I try to be as local as possible – trying out local cuisines, listening to local music, hanging out at local joints, using public transport as and when – I try to live the experience to the extent possible. Moving away from palace life has taught me a very crucial lesson that the world belongs equally to all.

Come to think of it, travel is quite an equalizer, pretty much like going to a naturopathy clinic, visiting a shrine or a temple.

Taking Lead

For all good reasons, I have thankfully been very independent and focussed in whatever I choose to undertake. On rare occasions, I have even asked myself if travel helped hone these skills, though most definitely the answer is no. But it has helped immensely. For any travel enthusiast, it is very intriguing to learn how other people plan their trips, what their primary must-dos on the travel checklist are. Excursions and travels at a younger age have the advantage of making one responsible; from travel documents and belongings to understanding immigration and international travel rules, it helps to prepare by reading up and researching on the destination. Eventually, you get richer by building better memories.

Connecting with Self

More often than not, packing bags and setting out has offered a wide spectrum of experiences, each one beating the previous in immediacy and novelty. Do you find yourself wondering about the kind of holiday or travel to undertake? Fast-paced places can be energy-boosters but quiet peaceful locales allow you to 'live' the moment. They are both very different experiences, but desirable nonetheless. Travel, on the whole, provides a certain inner quietude which is enhanced if one is journeying in the mountains or on water. The hills and oceans have a huge capacity to absorb one's thoughts and feelings, it is almost like a conversation where none speaks yet plenty is communicated. They offer solace and companionship, encouraging introspection and retrospection. Waves appear to draw you in and mountains promise to keep company. Each is therapeutic, depending on what suits the mood and moment then.

A Bit of Every Place Dwells in Me

There's something in me that changes a bit with every travel. What I am now is a fine amalgamation of the several travels I have been able to make. I am a seeker; I seek new learnings, new experiences, new cultures and new understandings. There is a bit we bring back with us from the places we visit and the people we encounter. The American way of life has taught me that everyone's opinion matters irrespective of age; the British have taught me poise and dignity, Japan tutored me in detailing skills and Africa prepared me to keep an open approach. From Singapore, I learnt discipline, from Russia, severity. China has taught me scale, Australia, to seek opportunities, Greece showed how warmth can be and India has taught me tolerance. Watching people, interacting with them and understanding their reasoning or point of view helps to delve into and understand human psychology as well. Otherwise, our vision would be very narrow, restricted to only what is physically visible or floating around us.

Beyond Mode

Often while traveling, though the destinations are important, it is the journey that leaves a lasting impression. I have used different modes of transport while travelling. Long drives with good music are truly fulfilling, but then, air travel is what I have undertaken most if I also consider business travels.

Then again, the scenic beauty and the peace and quiet that long train journeys provide, especially in Western countries, is unmatched. Nothing can equal the fun of travel in India with its wayside *dhabas* and restaurants. Luxury cruises are an experience in themselves, but they tempt you to overeat. Thankfully, I manage to walk enough during my trips, which is why holidays help me lose some weight and tone up, so I don't have to worry about extra kilos once I am back!

Adventure and Peace Trails

While planning our travels, we sometimes decide to get adventurous. At such times, trekking and biking becomes a favoured choice. But trekking or biking involves a lot more than you might be bargaining for; it is necessary to be fit and take into account oxygen levels, weather travails, etcetera while participating in long winding walks and uphill journeys.

Then there are adventure sports like skydiving, parasailing, snorkelling, skiing, which make you experience the world differently – at times like a free-spirited bird, at other times, an underwater creature. I am always game for whatever the destination has to offer.

I also make an annual trip to naturopathy centres to detoxify and get rejuvenated. I am conscious of my calorie intake when travelling, but other than that, I tend to go with the flow. Whatever the place has to offer, I happily seek and grab it.

Of the many things I have done, I feel great about having travelled to various parts of the world. Each place has its feel, but Kerala and Greece have felt like home. India and Greece, both have the honour of possessing really ancient civilisations.

As for Kerala, I feel I have roots there and each time I return from 'God's own country', there is an immense craving to go back. The tranquil backwaters and the charming houseboats are glued in memory; in Greece, it feels like being transported back in time… be it at the differently coloured beaches or the most photographed heritage sites, the old-fashioned cafes and the cobbled streets of the old towns. While Greece has drawn more than a couple of times, Kerala kept luring me many times over. Other memorable travels include my trip to the Baltic Area – Estonia and Lithuania, my holiday in Alaska and my expedition to Mount Kailash and Chardham, each of these hold an extremely special place in my memory.

The Best Teacher

I still clearly remember our holidays during childhood; these included going to Kolkata which was close to Odisha. Since I lived in a hostel, going home was such a delight that holidays outside of home didn't mean much. Staying home, relaxing and doing as one pleases was more of a holiday then. But we did travel to different cities to represent our school in sports events.

The joy of travelling with family, especially with the child, has been a different pitch altogether. Advait has travelled extensively with us since he was very young. He was treated as an equal; he was not only in charge of his luggage but also his packing and currency. Later, he would manage his add-on credit card too. As a parent, one wants a child to progress, in every which way. My son, who has travelled internationally since he was two, has a great sense of direction, better than his parents'. He once recounted an incident from his Grade

9 study tour where most people, including the accompanying teacher, were on their first trip abroad. He had helped in filling the immigration forms, managing passports, etcetera. Now, being a young man, he often travels alone with friends; as a parent, it is assuring to know he is in control of his life.

It is good for children to travel, with family and by themselves, as early as possible, for horizons to broaden. Travel gives shape and makes real all that they read in books or watch in moving pictures and films. It helps them make friends and become global citizens.

The Road Ahead

I have had many rich travel experiences, but what keeps life interesting are little desires one aims to fulfil. On my bucket list, places on priority are the Arctic region, Antarctica and the Land of Midnight Sun. The novelty of these places is beckoning and has lured many a traveller from different corners of the world. Why do people want to travel and experience something different? Why are they willing to step beyond their comfort zones? Perhaps because novelty pulls, and at the core of the human heart lies a desire to explore the unknown, the unseen. And there is nothing greater than travel when it comes to learning and growing.

Travel is the undisputed teacher, one that broadens your perspective and adds to your treasure trove of memories.

Travel to faraway lands, that's possibly where you will pick up bits of your own story.

Travel to
faraway lands,
that's possibly
where you will
pick up bits
of your own
story.

It is encouragement that works by and large, sometimes challenges do too. But role models and unseen forces can contribute to making wishes come true.

CHAPTER SIXTEEN

Led By Forces

Everyone is constantly learning, from something or someone, and feeling inspired, emulating, or embarking on a journey to create – be it a project or an enterprise, a home or a career. While personal knowledge, both inherent and acquired, could play a major role in planning ahead, executing and decision-making, there are unseen forces that have a major hand in the success of one's undertaking. It does not have to be a commercial, financial or social takeaway; sometimes emotional lessons and psychological understanding provide the much-needed encouragement to get you started.

For as long as I remember, I have relied heavily on myself for plans I have chalked out and decisions I have taken. However, as with all of us, there are some key forces that played their part in moulding me, even if by lack of design, by simply being around. Sometimes, big learnings and lessons lie in seemingly small and insignificant acts. Interestingly, you figure that out only with time and experience, when you look back to analyse how and what made you do what you eventually did.

I believe instinct and intuition play a major role in leading us to decisions we arrive at. And somewhere, our childhood and the people who impacted us most then, naturally have a hand therein. It is observations made, and results experienced back in those years, that go on to shape our thoughts, beliefs and ideologies. Also, we relate best to those that connect to some inherent part of our being, be it emotional, mental or practical.

Inspiration Begins at Home

All through childhood and subsequently while growing up, I remember having a natural curiosity towards things happening around me – from the minutest matters to the biggest of issues. And it isn't just me; I believe every child has an approach to viewing proceedings and concerns around them, absorbing and learning from them, only to subconsciously imbibe from them. I guess that happened with me as well.

Growing up, I never quite adored or worshipped anyone to the extent that I wanted to be like them, but yes, I did greatly admire and emulate my grand aunt, Didi. My mother called her so because she saw her mother address her thus. We all called her Didi; she was my grandmother's elder sister which is where the 'didi' originated from. I don't remember consciously seeing her as a role model though she was a very impressive individualistic person. But if a role model is someone who inspires, Didi definitely did so. If a role model is someone who encourages others to action, she surely did.

Impact and Impressions

Learning by observation is perhaps the best method. If someone is able to arrest your attention by the way they do something, it is likely to leave a lasting impression. Didi's dedication to getting a task done was extremely commendable. Her sense of commitment was such that once she decided to do something, nothing could stop her. She would go to any length to ensure it happened. I was particularly taken in by her passion and decision-making ability. In fact, as a young girl, I was impressed by her actions and remember trying to emulate her. Didi never quite went to school, but not being literate did not stop her from dealing with revenue, legal and financial issues. I am a chip off that block which is why not knowing something does not stop me. I believe I can always learn.

Actually, it is with her that the distinction between being literate and educated became clear to me at an early stage in life. Since children are influenced most by elders in the family, it greatly helps to have strong examples to follow. With strength comes confidence and conviction, both of which are great personality shapers.

There are always a few who leave stamps on our memory. Among those I remember is my Headmistress from school who was firm yet loving, my mentor in Delhi University who had terrific clarity of thought, several people at Kalorex from whom I have learnt the skill of detailing and to focus on processes, my investors who have taught me to keep an eye on the big picture and my husband who gets straight to the point.

Role Models and Positivity

In the early years, parents become role models for children, and it is possible that unconsciously they set wrong examples for their kids. It is very important to be aware – of what one says, what one does, what one follows, what one rejects. As parents or adults, we sometimes forget the watchful eyes of children and speak inappropriately. We are not mindful of what we utter, or perhaps are driven by the moment to do or say something, without realising it could be detrimental to the child's psychology and understanding. An example would be parents discussing guests after they have left. Children are keen observers of parental behaviours and mannerisms, therefore, one's integrity and synergy in thought, word and action is prerequisite to being a role model.

My Icon Growing Up

In our formative years, certain public figures deeply impress us and end up playing a role in building our personalities. Condoleezza 'Condi' Rice, the American diplomat, political scientist, civil servant, and professor who served as the 66th United States Secretary of State from 2005 to 2009 and as the 20th United States National Security Advisor from 2001 to 2005 is one such person. I have followed her life by reading up on her often. There is a quote on success I subscribe to, by an American author and educator Booker T Washington which says, 'Success is to be measured not so much by the position that one has reached in life as by the obstacles which one has overcome.' If one were to explore this statement alone, one can imagine what Condoleezza Rice would have overcome in her journey to become the first female African-American Secretary of State and the first woman to serve as National Security Advisor. Even imagining the opposition that she might have faced or paths she might have established, could reflect the journey that must have gone into shaping the person she became.

To be an Inspiration

Just as I was influenced and inspired by some people in my early years, today I feel humbled and a sense of pride when people look up to me as a source of inspiration. The world is definitely moving at a fast pace; information is available on fingertips and nothing seems unachievable anymore. In times such as these, it takes immense strength and focus to be an inspiration to the younger lot.

In our organisations, I have often had the opportunity to interact with young girls who are not only excited to follow what is shared with them but particularly look up to lessons learnt from the life of their educator.

I once had a grade 11 girl student say she wanted to be like me, 'always surrounded by people, someone who can get a job done by simply snapping her fingers'. This may be far from the truth, but knowing that someone sees you as one who can make things happen, is in itself empowering and motivating. You want to live up to inspire, you want to ensure you play your part well for a generation that looks up to you and who you may be responsible in shaping.

Often people only see the end result and not the hard work and learning that goes into it. Only I know how much time and effort goes into completing a task, from the drawing board stage to execution to the final result. Young students perhaps get such fleeting impressions, but then it is these impressions that home in on their minds, and lead them to desire and achieve more from their lives. Role models not only inspire but can also be a driving force in achieving what one puts sight and might on.

At Kalorex, when staff members tell me they are inspired and motivated by my hard work and visionary ideas, my nerves of steel when it comes to dealing with difficult situations, my capacity to withhold pressure and act with some semblance of normalcy when the chips are down, I am spurred to do better so I can live up to their expectations.

Leading from the Front

I have never waited for others to act upon a matter that requires my attention. I would rather demonstrate leadership by going first. At times, you have to initiate and crack the tough part for others to gain confidence and follow. Demonstrating is more effective than explaining or commanding. As a leader you ought to take the first step in order to give confidence to your team. I lead from the front; hopefully I am creating the right impressions for people who might consider me a role model. I am, after all, responsible for shaping a thought process, a confidence mantra and a young mind that will eventually deal with the highs and lows of life as per its initial few experiences and impressions.

Learnings are impressions on memory. What we absorb will reveal itself through what we give out.

A trek in the mountains, or a swim in the ocean, a walk in the woods works too. Chase the outdoors, play some games, no reason to ever feel blue.

CHAPTER SEVENTEEN

Out In The Open

What good is life if it does not give you some comforting moments in the lap of nature, embracing tranquillity, every once a while? A chase to the mountain top or a walk in the woods, some song and dance to cheer you up, a bit of this and a bit of that is what keeps alive the joie de vivre. When it comes to outdoor activities, there is no dearth of desires; while some carry a poet's soul, soaking in the vast expanse around them, the thrill of adventure lures others. Parasailing over clear waters could be stress-busting, while an undersea walk, a soothing yet lively experience.

The outdoors has a strong impact on our system, both mentally and physically; I realised that long ago, perhaps when I was still in school. There is an all-encompassing feeling of joy about being outdoors, a thrilling feeling. Outdoor and adventure sports are energy boosters that never fail to de-stress the soul.

Nature Lover

I've always been a city girl, even realised my dreams and aspirations in the city, but part of my heart is unfailingly and eternally partial to the mountains, the forests, the flowing rivers. It is where I go to for solace, to deal with issues and to think more clearly, to find strength and revitalise myself, to ponder and question, to find answers and to recharge.

Nature has a unique quality – while its offerings remain the same for all, each person's takeaway varies as per their thinking, priority and interaction. A mountain view could offer more joy than a ride in a fancy car; the waves of the sea could be more comforting than a palatial home. It is not for nothing that nature is known to be the greatest revitalizer. Getting in touch or allowing oneself to sync with nature is a step towards self-realisation and untold joy. There are thoughts within and vibrations beyond that amalgamate to create serenity that is unparalleled. It is in the quietude of nature that you lose your concerns; it is the calmness of nature that enables you to de-stress, and the lap of nature where you find the true meaning and value of abundance. Nothing equals being around flowing waters, amid green expanses of luscious forests, or under vast open skies dotted with clouds. In fact, even imagining yourself in such spaces is comforting.

Always in for Outdoors

While the cosiness of home is unequalled, the charm of the outdoors carries its own pull. I strongly believe the outdoors can heal and cure. Being out in the open is known to make people feel livelier and sharper, yet calmer and more relaxed. The ability to absorb the surroundings and feel one with nature comes in especially when you are surrounded by endless plants and trees, streams and rivers, hills and vast terrains. An outdoor person will invariably be of happier disposition; he will value the freedom that being out in the open gives to the mind and the body.

Experiencing and recognising the vastness of the earth and its relation to the Milky Way make all problems pertaining to life and living seem miniscule, almost insignificant in context. The sense of abundance, be it the expanse of the sky or the vastness of the ocean, the unending mountains or the wildlife nestled amidst deep jungles, nature is a reminder of everything magnanimous. I firmly believe life must be lived in abundance and nature unfailingly reminds me of this philosophy of abundance. The abundant mentality in turn allows love, resources and opportunities to blossom in life.

More and more frequently, I have seen amazing changes in people who embrace the outdoors. As for myself, it has made me happier and healthier. Outdoors means less stress, more concentration, increased exposure to sunlight, which is a temperament booster. Being outdoors has particularly seen me get out of my comfort zone, it has helped me explore and has pushed me to my limits. Outdoors have helped me confront my fears, they have built my muscles and my character.

Being Sporty

If being in the lap of nature can be soothing and calming, it can also be energetic and lively. I recall running marathons and participating in cycling races. I have tried my hand at parasailing and skydiving, snorkelling and skiing. I have trekked and walked long distances. Be it on land, air or water, I have tried all kinds of sports activities only to realise the more of these in life the merrier it is. While some sports leave you tired and breathless in the moment, they impart a tremendous feel-good factor a few minutes later. The sense of achievement sporty encounters provide is something I wouldn't trade for anything.

I distinctly recall my skydiving experience, it was pretty unbeatable and unforgettable. We went skydiving as a family in New Zealand. The idea of jumping off a plane is so frightening that I almost backed out of it. But since everyone in the family was doing it, including my son who was not even ten, and my husband who always encourages me to confront my fears, I just went for it. I think sitting on the edge of the plane ready to jump off is the most gripping feeling one can experience. But as you sail down, the joy and freedom is unmatched too. From the fresh air rushing against the face to feeling free like a bird, from watching everything miniscule to experiencing the vastness of the world from up there, this sporty escapade was an exhilarating experience with extraordinary feelings and sensations that don't come by too often.

As a family, we have always chosen sporty vacations over mere luxury, especially mountaineering, since Pratul is a great trekker. Advait, in fact, has been trekking since he was two years old. Our travels across Europe and Australia involved plenty of walking. I am not mentioning the USA as a holiday destination since Pratul and Advait treat it as a place of work.

We have only taken family holidays and never been on group holidays. Our vacations have been typically about finding one exotic location and walking around it. This is less stressful, since for us it isn't about covering places, but enjoying the one you choose to be in. The thrill and joy of being together is doubled in these beautiful locales, each one unique and yet part of one vast expanse.

My Have-To List

For as long as I can remember, I have been a daily exercise person. It could be practicing yoga or sweating it out at the gym or even outdoor activities like cycling, jogging or simply walking. I like to observe little things around, especially when I am by myself with little to disturb. Registering sounds is also an interest, be it a bird cooing, a squirrel nibbling, a dog barking, a bee humming, a child giggling or even a large group of people laughing.

Since I am an avid dancer, I set aside a few hours for dance every week. It is relaxing, fun and rejuvenation all together. During the lockdown, I reconnected with singing and put in a few hours of practice every week. Excitement and therapy, it has offered both.

Taking Indoors Outside

Apart from our primary work and interest, it is hobbies and other artistic pursuits that make life more fulfilling. They are an integral part of one's personality and every person has an inclination towards some activity or interest. I like to believe that one expresses one's innermost self through these interests.

In our organisation we have hobby clubs so people can find self-expression along with professional productivity. Outdoor hobbies and interests are even better; they can be great mood supplements.

I am more of an outdoor person; this is apparent not just in trips I undertake, but in my daily engagements as well. Pratul,

Advait and his cousins can play board games for hours at a stretch but I am simply not that person. I do not understand the art of playing cards and associated games. I have never taken a fancy to video games, nor have digital games ever enticed me.

It makes me very happy to say that I am both, a singer and a dancer; these are the best pastimes in my regular diary of events. Both these forms of performing arts are unique, distinct and varied. Dance is about the self, expressing through the face, eyes, hands, feet and body, while, in singing, you simply use your vocal cords to communicate a wide range of emotions – from fun, joy and exuberance to sadness, anger and strife. While both are power-packed activities indoors, the element of these in the outdoors elevates not just the mood but also the art therein. The abundance and openness of nature and its surroundings make these experiences a lot richer, a lot deeper.

I have been dancing since my school days. I used to be a favourite with my dance teachers and always played lead roles in all classical dance recitals. There is no formal training in dance but being from Odisha, I was taught Odissi in school. I still have fond memories of playing a strong character in 'Black Swan' and the Sun God in 'Konark', both classic dance dramas. As a way to mark respect and reverence for this Indian classical dance form, I promoted Odissi classical dance classes here in Gujarat and these Odissi dance students have performed at the Modhera Dance Festival. Odissi is a less known form of classical dance in Western India and very few tutors pass on this art. I am glad to be part of promoting this dance form in Gujarat.

So, while watching others dance supplements joy, the experience I undergo when dancing is unparalleled. I love dance to the extent I wouldn't miss it even if unwell. Truth is dancing perks me up, the adrenaline rush makes me more active and happy. The act of dancing releases happy hormones in me.

Music to My Ears

Music has made the world go round for people across the globe. There are times I ask myself if I am a singer first or a dancer. I seem to enjoy both tremendously and have every inclination to ensure I keep up with both forever. I think singing for me began very young. I remember people around me – relatives and family friends – prompting me to sing. And then of course in school I was quite popular as a singer where my school buddies highly rated my voice texture and swore by my voice quality. After marriage and child-birth, I kind of completely got caught up with striking a work and home balance and somewhere along the way, lost touch with singing.

But compliments weren't hard to come by, even when I hummed or sang a few lines. I did consider learning Hindustani classical formally but that was a challenge since I travelled very frequently.

However, a few years ago, some friends started a karaoke group and provided me the opportunity to sing. The lockdown further gave me some earnest time to get back to singing and I am thoroughly enjoying reconnecting with my old singing self.

The only connection that matters is the one with the cosmos. The best way to achieve this is via meditation which could be tough; the easier way to establish a higher connection is through music.

I looked at life with joy, and wrapped my arms around it; there were some rocky patches and bumpy rides, but it never let me down.

CHAPTER EIGHTEEN

Free-Flowing And Forever Young

There is no such thing as forever, and yet forever is such a hopeful, beautiful and strength-inducing word. We often use it in random everyday musings, when understanding the present vis-a-vis permanence, when expressing love, when buying things, when making vital plans, and more so when nailing key decisions. Living in the moment can guarantee joy forever; although an antithetical expression, it is loaded with immense promise. And while we think and talk about permanence, it helps when we believe that staying happy and young or staying focussed and resilient forever is possible – for it is in the approach we take and the outlook we possess.

My zest for life has been enormous, often leading me to things that not only have uplifted my path but been great boosters in everything else I have undertaken. Besides leading an active and outdoorsy life, it is yoga that has been a constant motivator of sorts, a strong preserver of the self; it has brought about an apparent change, felt more within than outside.

Perhaps playing sports, be it basketball or kabaddi, during school years, and being an avid cyclist, trekker and marathoner in the years that followed, contributed in keeping the spirits high and the cheerfulness and youthfulness unscathed. Other factors that keep life's fascination flowing have included sky-diving, parasailing, skiing, each one ensuring buoyancy in spirit and gratification to brighten the inner light. Outdoor activities besides releasing dopamine, the feel-good hormone, in a certain way maintain youthfulness in life and induce a feeling of being a liberated unbridled spirit.

Relying on the Self

Life is sure to bring in a variety of experiences, some beautiful, some complex and others challenging. There are bound to be tough hurdles, delayed successes and everything that justifies life to be a roller coaster, but how we handle it is clearly in our control. We need to understand and be aware that everything in life is an experience to be lived, and endured. It does not have to knock you down. I remember reading this: What is outside cannot be controlled, but what is inside, can be. Life is a mirror reflecting our inner world. So, by getting in touch, relying and trusting our core being, by following the voice within, we can enhance our life. External circumstances will change in the way they are meant to, what we can do is take control of the reactions. A balanced outlook and approach can resolve most issues. There is no point in getting riled while biding time for external conditions to resolve. It won't hasten the solution; if anything, it can create interferences and harm the process.

Being strongly connected to your inner self will allow the internal condition to guide the external. My belief system and my lifestyle have been my major influencers. Indeed, like many of us, I do have trusted friends in whose hands I have placed my life and wellness, who definitely have provided rock solid support and greatly helped the journey so far.

What's Inside is Outside

That age is merely a number, is an oft repeated quote, a very popular belief all over the world. I am also a strong endorser of this belief. Especially inspired by Ray Kurzweil and Deepak Chopra, I feel there is no such thing as ageing process. As a matter of fact, figuratively speaking, age can be reversed. While there is wear and tear of organs and body parts, by practising alternative medical science, specifically the ancient science of Ayurveda, one can rebuild youthfulness in all aspects, thereby reversing the ageing process.

I recall doing *yogasanas* during my teenage years, and no, it wasn't something I learnt from a yoga guru, but simply by looking at magazines and articles published therein. Nobody introduced me to or taught me yoga; I simply got drawn to it by looking at pictures which I would attempt to imitate. I was able to do almost all the mid-degree asanas without any hitch or difficulty. I liked doing yoga since it made me feel rejuvenated though it is only much later that I read books and understood the importance of yoga and its benefits.

Daily regimen of this practice in the form of exercises with a dedicated instructor is a recent phenomenon, but interest and understanding of yoga in my life has been largely inherent and natural. I am sure it is a path I was destined to walk on.

Staying Calm is Life Balm

Like I said, it all starts in the head. That holds true not just for the positive and good things in life but also the negative ones. Keeping the mind relaxed and calm can ease tensions and problems that may come up from time to time. I remember being diagnosed with hypothyroidism while I was living in Delhi and was advised medication. Being told it was a lifelong condition made it seem big but I don't think I understood details back then. Something within had me believe that no condition could be permanent and incurable. I simply wasn't convinced that I'd have to resort to medication to control my thyroid functions for the rest of my life. I felt sure there was a way out, a way to deal with this and reverse the condition. I turned to books and began reading, which is when I found *pranayama* and breathing exercises for thyroid. That apart, wearing a positive attitude, 'talking to' and healing the organ helped. I have never had to bank upon medication thereafter.

The Mind-Gut Connection

What is your gut feeling? Haven't we heard that several times, especially when taking a decision or finalising something? It is commonly referred to as a feeling derived from an emotional and instinctive response as opposed to calculated thought or decision. And like they say, gut is the second brain. Both the brains are closely associated with each other and hence treating one can treat the other. Gut-related issues including indigestion or irritable bowel syndrome could cause mental fogginess and vice versa. Various other mental conditions like depression can play havoc on the gut digestion. An increasing number of people across the globe are waking up to better understanding of the central role that digestion plays in preserving mental health.

Ageing vs Healing

Everyone wants to slow the ageing process, but hasten the healing process. Well, that said, it is true that we all want to delay the process of ageing, if for nothing else than to enjoy good health for a little longer. The average life span today has increased; people could live well into their eighties. Instead of approaching ageing with a sense of alarm, it is important to understand the role of natural healing in the process of ageing gracefully and with dignity.

Our body is a complex mass made up of life energy that runs through subtle pathways and meridians. At the centre are the seven chakras. Healing is a way of stimulating and unblocking these meridians such that our natural energy can flow easily and restore the natural balance of the body. There are many natural healing mechanisms which include third eye chakra healing, acupressure, reiki, acupuncture, reflexology, homeopathy, naturopathy and many more. These are known to benefit the human mind and body in ways that seem impossible at first. But when embraced, they rarely disappoint. They have not only cured but have borne unbelievable results.

Body Types Matter

Not everyone you speak to may understand the meaning and benefits of knowing one's body type. But it surely is an interesting subject where prioritising health and related matters are concerned. There are a few theories that categorise bodies as per the blood type and prescribe foods that agree with a certain blood type. There are, therefore, recommendations for

Type O, Type A, Type B and Type AB.

The ancient Indian alternative medicine, the science of Ayurveda, classifies people into categories of *vata, pitta, kapha,* and subsequent to these as *vata-pitta, vata-kapha* and *pitta-kapha*. Ayurveda recommends food and exercises according to these body types and even suggests common ailments that could arise if a person predominantly belongs to any of these.

A well-curated diet is about eating the right kind of food. And to those who understand this, the body is bound to remain in a state of balance and harmony.

Connecting to One's Higher Self

Emotional, mental and physical stability is key to a healthy and well-balanced life. Emotional stability can only come when you discern that the life force or the soul within is distinct from the physical body. Understanding the journey of the soul sets apart a person in their approach and reaction to life's situations. How you view things that happen to you and around you, by and large, decides how happy or sad, affected or unaffected you will be.

No Pill, Only Will

The bigger the crisis, the larger the process of dealing with it. Life is not always smooth sailing; a sudden crisis throws everything off-gear. At such times, there is no option but to deal with it. Someone once asked me how many sleeping pills I have to resort to while getting through crisis situations, that have struck me quite repeatedly in life. The question actually got me thinking since I have never had to seek solace in sleeping pills, not even during international travel to accommodate time zones. Dealing with stress and crisis is more about thinking and executing a plan that finds a way out; I definitely would not take sleeping pills for that. Perhaps my belief in the larger good, along with my faith, has helped me face strong winds. Coupled with this is logic that allows better reasoning to prevail.

Gratitude and Call of the Soul

It isn't a recent or developed thought process; I have always been a firm believer in the journey of the soul. My vision is focussed on multiple lives. When one has singular focus on the present lifetime, certain things and experiences appear larger than life, perhaps unreasonable, unfair and illogical too. But when one thinks about multiple lives with focus on different experiences and the journey of the soul, this material existence and all that comes with it falls into perspective.

Also, a big factor that can turn the wheel of life is gratitude. It is perhaps the greatest trait one can have; it is a positive disposition that can instantly change the complexity of any situation. Gratitude anchors a person, makes one look at the sunny side and protects them from harmful, negative thoughts. Gratitude also helps you create a strong connection with the mighty universe. Over a period of time, I have seen and understood how the benefits of practising gratitude in thought, action and speech stay unmatched.

Only a Pause, Never a Fullstop

Life has thrown endless challenges at me, perhaps that has been nature's way of preparing me for a detached existence. Each time there has been a setback, I have focussed singularly on getting back on track. It may sound a tad philosophical, but the only way ahead is moving forward. When challenges are immense in nature, it can be very time and energy consuming, but right intentions eventually iron things out. If anything, I have stood my ground, been honest in every action and speech, believing truth will eventually prevail.

Comebacks after setbacks, this has also been my primary guiding thought. Life is like a hurdle race. Just as you need good nutrition and physical endurance to keep crossing hurdles, each one more challenging than the previous one, in life's journey, to face challenges that come by, one needs a balanced emotional outlook with deep-rooted faith and conviction as preparatory tools to march ahead.

Down but not Out

In life, there are many a times when your chips are down – when things don't go your way, when there seems to be negativity all around, when the odds are stacked against you, when the light at the end of the tunnel is not even flickering, when situations are terrifying. It is during these times that it becomes important to remember the morning sun, which reminds us that every day is a new day and that new beginnings are possible.

Closing a Few Doors

I am a very sincere person when it comes to building lasting relationships. Altercations could be roadblocks when dealing with people by and large, but they have to be overcome, especially when the relationship is important and meaningful. However, there are a few doors that must be closed. These doors are not shut owing to pride or arrogance, but simply because these doors lead nowhere. We often find ourselves in situations with people where we believe we have given our best to the relationship, in terms of time, energy and emotion, and yet it yields no growth or betterment. It could also drain our energy or make us feel unworthy and unimportant. And yet our heart and mind wishes to pursue them. That is precisely when you need to understand that some doors are better closed, since they don't lead you anywhere.

Sharing SHROFFism

Observing and absorbing from life around can be a great teacher. Over the years, from my college days in Odisha to working in Delhi to coming to Ahmedabad and escalating my entrepreneurial journey, there is a lot of learning I have accumulated through experiences, people, situations and new platforms. Wanting to share this hard-gained knowledge, I started Shroffism videos for social media platforms in response to the queries I received, asking me how I maintain my energy levels or manage to remain youthful. This is a holistic science that involves the mind, body and soul. It is a physical, mental and spiritual journey where you cannot pick and work on one area alone while ignoring the others. They are all connected and intertwined and are bound to each other. Through Shroffism, I began sharing information on wellness, lifestyle and habits, keeping it short and crisp, as attention span is getting shorter by the day. These brief messages in the form of videos allow me to communicate, share information and spread awareness on subjects that have mass appeal, and more importantly, those that stand to benefit a larger tribe.

A strong core is bound to sustain you, no matter what flows by.

You seek and you find, believe and get aligned. Some paths lead you to others, and that is where you eventually discover yourself.

CHAPTER NINETEEN

The Light Within

What really educates and enlightens you is the experiences you have had or the experiences you have heard about. While your experiences exclusively allow you to seek, undergo and soak in; listening to rich, varied and studied experiences enhance your world view, especially those coming from learned minds that see everything with a generous mix of awareness, understanding and reason.

Meetings with Saints

It has been my good fortune to be able to meet quite a few learned men, scholars and saints who have walked the earth during my lifetime. As a teen, I have memories of spiritual discourses, *satsangs* as they are popularly known, held at houses of relatives who were followers of Chinmaya Mission. At our palace, every festival was celebrated with a corresponding puja and ritual. As I grew up, I developed a natural inclination to the world beyond this material plane; my quest made me turn to tons of literature written on this subject. Being a spiritual seeker, I have had the good fortune of meeting a few saints, including Sri Ravi Shankar, Ma Amritanandamayi, Sadhguru Jaggi Vasudev, His Divine Holiness Bhagawan Nithyananda Paramahamsa.

The Guru will Find You

While each of us has the capacity to look within and find our purpose, besides charting our journeys, life finds profound meaning with a guru, a teacher, a mentor, to guide you. A guru can, for example, remove in you the fear of death and very simply explain how death is like moving from one room into another. Legend has it that Sharada Devi was in deep anguish when her husband Sri Ramakrishna Paramahamsa died; she was removing her bangles as per the ritual widows follow, when Sri Ramakrishna's vision appeared, saying, 'I have not passed away, I have gone from one room to another.'

A guru takes you from darkness to light, leads you from ignorance to knowledge. And while the guru can help connect to the God within, the guru also guides you inward, outward and forward towards God; how one utilises, imbibes, internalises and assimilates the guru's teachings depends on every individual spiritual seeker and aspirant.

Having said that, it is also very important to make a distinction between a guru's teachings and the life of the guru on earth. The teachings of the guru are food and fodder for the soul. The instructions, the simplicity and clarity with which ancient wisdoms are communicated, opens up the spiritual path for the seeker, whereas the life, mission and purpose of the guru in the mortal form is best known only to their wisdom and their inner self.

Connecting with the God within will take you towards a life of discipline, allowing you to live dispassionately and with no discrimination. It will gift you liberation, supplement joy and provide bliss, no matter what the circumstances.

Finding the Formless in the Form

What exactly does a form do? It provides you with an image that establishes further reading, understanding and absorption of the meaning you attach to it. God in a form encourages belief and sustains confidence. The form lets you construct meaning; it gifts you the ability to bead together your beliefs and thoughts meticulously. And yet, it is ironical that the very form we see and associate deep meaning and faith with, is actually formless so to say. None of us have 'seen' God and yet we 'feel' Him around. We associate with the form and find strength in knowing that God guides us, that God is watching over us, that God is supreme energy. We believe that we are guided and loved, that there is someone who can crack the code the rest of us are alien to. We trust that the energy we receive from our belief in God will carry us through our troubles, big and small. It is in the form we see that we actually comprehend the formless. And it is this formless strength that sails us through every phase of our life.

Spirituality Brings Trials

Faith and spirituality, be they in any form, tend to bring in upheavals. History has borne testimony to the fact that spirituality begets extreme trials. Enlightened higher souls have had to walk through fire during their mortal existence on earth. Each one of us is born on earth to fulfil our *prarabdha* which Swami Sivananda explains as 'that portion of the past karma which is responsible for the present body'. I have come to the conclusion that there is great power to change, and great transformation lies in the many unexplained and inexplicable trials that are bestowed upon us by the cosmos. These trials often test our character as also the grounds and roots of our faith in God and godliness. These trials could be of short or long duration; they could be mental, physical, plain emotional or even extraneous to oneself, they may occur once or could have repeated occurrence. Trials often come as obstacles and setbacks to our obvious and visible progress in the life that we are born to. As a spiritual seeker, I would look at these circumstances and trials as a test to build strength of character, to have understanding far deeper than the surface level, and with a belief that trials have a specific purpose of building maturity within us. Trials are ultimately the fuel that reignite our passion and dedication to continue our journey as a spiritual seeker.

Are Trials a Blessing?

Everything seems overwhelming when one is undergoing a difficult experience. When one is going through trials, strife and trauma, it is easy to slip into a delusional patch that prompts you to believe life is unfair. You may even begin to question divinity or wonder if trials are a sign that God is angry, that he is punishing you by making you undergo whatever tribulation you might be facing. My contention, on the contrary, is that trials are to be recognised as opportunities for deeper and clearer understanding. Often our spiritual growth and prayers bring upon us trials that will help propel our faith to the next higher level, thus helping us up our karma chart.

Just as everything in life has a reason, a meaning, all pain and trials have a purpose. One of the toughest things to do while going through hardships is to remain rooted in faith and to believe that trials are not a sign of God's wrath. Difficult as it may seem for us to believe, we are not experiencing hardship because God is angry with us, or wants us to learn a lesson, rather He is inculcating a loving discipline in us. Simply said, it is like God wants us to pass an exam and hence presents a question paper. We may find it tough, but it gives us the opportunity to understand the question and answer it to the best of our knowledge and ability. Trials are, in fact, an approval from God; they are not an objection or a disapproval.

Trials Increase Faith

If faith diminishes or is questioned during trials, then sadly it was only surface deep. It is while facing the heat of trials and surmounting them that our hearts get purified. Trials generate and build maturity, reinforce our perseverance, build strength of character and support unshaken faith.

Trials are God's approval of our spiritual journey; trials are not obstacles but are bridges that bring you closer to your destination by refuelling, reigniting and rekindling your growth. Enduring trials with increased faith is passing a spiritual exam. If you have learnt and grown, you will move to a higher level.

Reading books, scriptures and sacred writings is known to improve understanding, however, at times they may seem confusing to an early seeker. Deep wisdom can be unfathomable. A spiritual master who can decipher these scriptures and communicate with ease can be a guiding force to any spiritual seeker.

Experiencing Happiness

The feeling of pure happiness is often considered sublime and invaluable. Be it from external things or from peace within, deep happiness can make you feel ecstatic, gratified and even unreal. It is perhaps true that people who seek happiness may never find it. After all, it is elusive, more so if you search for it outside, in things, people or situations. What you possibly need to do is listen to the voice within. What is inside is largely projected outside, so if you are at peace and feel content within, external happiness is yours to keep. But if you are restless and insecure within, happiness may seem obscure. Getting rid of misery, pain and suffering can only happen when there is bliss, peace and tranquillity within you.

Simply put, the source of wisdom, the source of truth, the source of liberation, all lies within. The voice within is the God within. Since accessing this God has been challenging, across time and age, great spiritual masters, scholars and gurus, guide and mentor disciples are on this path of looking inward and connecting with the God within. This journey may be desirable to many, but perhaps less than one per cent of humanity is able to acquire the right knowledge and find the path to self-liberation.

Human birth is the most celebrated of all lives, since it is in this birth that God can be realised. Perhaps that is why it has been said that even Gods envy the human race. It is this race that can enjoy life to its maximum potential. Unfortunately, not many people understand or appreciate that human birth is an extraordinary gift that should be cherished and celebrated. The sooner mankind were to understand this, the better this world could be. It is important to instil this understanding in children early on in their life. Parents and teachers must help them get in touch with their inner voice or the God within. For rather than torturing the God within and ourselves with misery and pain arising from negative feelings of jealousy, comparison, anger, resentment and hatred, it is important to focus on positivity such as acceptance, surrender, joy, self-love, calmness and balance in thoughts.

Cheerleading Myself

Meditation and mantra-chanting help maintain inner calm, while absolute faith in God helps me stay afloat when handling situations of extreme nature, whatever be their magnitude. Regret is an emotion I don't indulge in. I have seen more than a fair share of hardships in my life, but I am not sorry for any part of it. Of course, I do wish life could have been more smooth sailing and less tumultuous, but still there are no deep regrets. I have always managed to pick up the threads, learn from the past and move on.

Whatever challenges life may throw up, one ought to be able to cheer the self and move past them. I possess a free soul, one that has clarity about its journey towards God. My soul feels liberated, and my internal state mirrors my external one. Life-changing episodes have created havoc; these instances have reinforced my belief in karma. I have been caught in a vortex of situations that I neither created nor was responsible for. People close to me, who I have known for several years, changed colours in times of trouble. However, rather than blame them, I choose to believe that people reacted to the situation rather than to me.

Finding Purpose

While death continues to remain a mystery, there are in-depth questions related to the real purpose of life. Would it be correct to say that the purpose of one's life is to make a name, revel in fame, accumulate wealth, acquire power, build the most gorgeous bungalow, buy the dream car, travel around the world, have a successful career, marry someone desirable and bear beautiful children? And if the purpose is to achieve all this, what is the point, since it will all eventually be gone. Finding purpose in all that you do lends meaning to life, it gives you a sense of direction. But ultimately you wonder if purpose is important or experiencing all that comes by is.

Approach to Living

It is the inner voice and the God within who has unfailingly risen and guided me through ups and downs, thick and thin. It is also this voice that has helped me keep my balance during strong currents when situations have seemed out of hand and the going got tough. I have especially experienced how crucial and severe even mild setbacks could seem when you are down and out, but being aware of one's feelings, actions and moves at that point is paramount. That is because you don't want any action to be a reaction to the moment and spoil your karma cycle. For it isn't in life itself that you experience the good and bad. It goes beyond, which is why it is even more imperative we think before we say or do something. Like they say, karma catches up.

Karmic Strength

The theory of karma forms the basic premise of my core belief: What has to be, will be, and we have little control over external situations and occurrences. I also hold the conviction of having done no wrong, which is why I feel confident that nothing bad will near me. And in case it does, it will pass away, leaving me with a lesson in the process. It does seem logical to believe in the Law of Karma, which, if simply put, refers to Newton's third law of motion – 'Every action will have an equal and opposite reaction.' The difference is that Newton's laws of motion refer to physical objects, and the Law of Karma refers to good and bad deeds, the credit balance of which is carried by the soul to the astral plane and further to the next birth. The theory of karma is like a balance sheet that keeps track of the good and bad deeds of a soul across multiple lifetimes. There is an opening balance at the time of birth and one's deeds accumulate points through the good and the bad undertaken as life progresses. At the point of death, karmic records are updated to be carried forward to the next birth. Quite like a credit-debit entry or a net profit-loss ratio where profit is akin to good deeds and loss to negative or bad deeds; the karmic cycle keeps a record of everything.

The soul never dies; it never meets an end. It resurfaces, into a new body, for a new journey of karmic settlements.

Life after Death

It is not something I heard from anyone as a child, neither do I have any distinct memory of reading about it in my teenage years, but I seem to inherently believe there is life after death. I felt that way as a young girl, and my faith has only strengthened with passing years. I have been a spiritual practitioner for as long as I remember and besides *mantra-jaap, puja, homa*, meditation, healing, I also practise spiritual channelling. That I am a spiritual seeker first, above all else, is something that is apparent not just to my immediate folks but also to those I interact with on a regular basis. Being a spiritual seeker by no means denies one of worldly pursuits, material aspirations or goals. It is the degree of detachment for material accomplishments that determines your spiritual quotient.

The quest for knowledge of the soul's journey post death is an eternal question. As a child I would wonder with limited knowledge, as an adult I continue to do so despite being armed with plenty of knowledge from books and attending discourses. What happens after one dies and discards the physical body? Where do we go once the heart stops beating? Why do we learn and accumulate so much when it takes only a second for us to be unhitched from everything? We don't quite know where we come from and certainly do not know where we will go after death. There is a hand above, the Creator, or God as most people call Him, who writes our story. To me He exists, and the ultimate journey remains the search for Him, for God, the Creator. Not only in life, but even after death.

Since this journey is so individualised, knowledge can be attained only through experience, no amount of theory can provide complete understanding of 'life' and 'death'.

Though almost everyone believes in the existence of the soul, questions remain –What is it? Is it immortal? Where is the proof? There is no scientific evidence to prove it. Then there are questions regarding heaven and hell; if there is a soul, where does it go after the body dies? We also do not have an answer to this. Perhaps there is an astral plane or the spirit world… and maybe it is in this spirit world that the soul rests, but who can prove it?

Fear of death is actually fear of life. Pack your bags, live in the moment and stay ready to take the final flight, any second.

GLOSSARY

A

Advait: Son of Manjula Pooja Shroff, an analyst and investor.

AI: Artificial Intelligence.

Amdavadi: One who is typical of Ahmedabad, the largest city of Gujarat.

Amy Poehler: American actress, comedian, writer, producer and director.

Asanas: Body postures ideal for meditation purpose.

Ayurveda: It is an alternative medicine system with historical roots in India.

B

Barsaati: A habitable room on the top floor of a building.
Below Poverty Line: An economic benchmark related to threshold income.

Board exams: Exams conducted at the end of class X and XII.

C

Centre for Professional Development in Higher Education: An institute in Delhi that provides opportunities for professional and career development to teachers across Indian universities.

CEO: Chief Executive Officer.

Connaught Place: A commercial and financial hub in the capital city of New Delhi, now renamed as Rajiv Chowk.

Cuttack: A city in Odisha, a state in eastern India.

D

Deepak Chopra: An Indian-American author and alternative medicine advocate.

Delhi: A city in northern India, also the capital territory.

Delhi Public School: A Central Board of Secondary Education school that first started in Delhi but now has branches across India.

Delhi University, North Campus: There are thirteen colleges hosted by the North Campus of Delhi University that was founded in 1922.

Dhabas: Small wayside and highway food joints usually on the outskirts of a village/town/city.

Didi: Grandaunt of Manjula Pooja Shroff, Rani Srimati Devi was affectionately addressed thus.

DNA: Abbreviation for deoxyribonucleic acid, it is the molecule inside cells that contains the genetic information responsible for the development and function of an organism. It is DNA molecules that allow this information to be passed from one generation to the next.

DTC buses: Delhi Transport Corporation buses, a public transport company.

E

Enid Blyton: A children's writer whose books have been among the world's bestsellers since the 1930s.

ERP: Enterprise Resource Planning.

F

Famous Five: A series of children's adventure novels and short stories by writer Enid Blyton.

Florence Nightingale: An English social reformer and statistician, she was the founder of modern nursing.

G

Garba: A traditional dance of Gujarat, especially performed during the nine-night festival of Navratri.

Gujarat: A state in the western part of India.

Guru: A revered teacher.

Guru-Shishya Parampara: It denotes a succession of teachers

and disciples in traditional vedic culture and Indian-origin religions such as Hinduism, Jainism, Sikhism and Buddhism.

H

Homa: A fire ritual performed on special occasions by a Hindu priest usually for a homeowner.

HR: Human Resources.

I

IIMA: Indian Institute of Management Ahmedabad.

Indian Institute of Management: A chain of Business Schools across India.

IT: Information Technology.

J

Jay Chandra Deo: Uncle of Manjula Pooja Shroff, her father's younger brother.

JEE: Joint Entrance Examination for admission to engineering colleges in India.

K

Kabaddi: A traditional Indian sport.

Kalorex: Under the banner of Kalorex Foundation, the Kalorex Group has several educational institutions across India.

Karmabhoomi: The earth is understood as a plane where you perform deeds and earn their consequences.

K12: A short form for the publicly-supported school grades prior to college These grades are kindergarten (K) and the 1st through the 12th grade.

L

Land of Midnight Sun: A land where sunset merges into sunrise. Norway is popularly known as the Land of Midnight Sun.

Louis Kahn Plaza: A section of Indian Institute of Management in Ahmedabad, named after architect of the same name. Louis Kahn designed the IIMA in 1974.

M

Make in India: It is an initiative by the Government of India to make and encourage companies to develop, manufacture and assemble products made in India.

Malory Towers: A series of six novels by children's writer Enid Blyton. The series is based on a girls' boarding school that Blyton's daughter attended, Benenden School, which relocated during the war to the Cornish seaside.

Mahatma Gandhi: Mohandas Karamchand Gandhi, popularly addressed as the Mahatma, was an Indian lawyer, anti-colonial nationalist, who employed non-violent ways to fight for India's freedom from British rule.

Manjula Manjari Devi: Parents of Manjula Pooja Shroff christened her with this name.

Manoja Manjari Devi: Elder sister of Manjula Pooja Shroff, politician from Odisha.

Mantra-Jaap: Chanting of holy verses and hymns.

Mills and Boons: A company that publishes romantic novels about relationships between men and women.

Modhera Dance Festival: An annual dance festival, also known as Uttarardh Mahotsav, held on the premises of Sun Temple at Modhera, Gujarat.

Mount Kailash: It is a 6,638 m high peak in the Kailash Range, which forms part of the Transhimalaya in the Ngari Prefecture, Tibet Autonomous Region, China. Mount Kailash is considered sacred in four religions that include Hinduism, Bon, Buddhism and Jainism.

N

National Institute of Design: A Design college based at Ahmedabad, Gandhinagar and Bangalore.

Naughtiest Girl: A series of novels written by children's writer Enid Blyton, set at a progressive boarding school rather than a traditional one.

Navratri: A Hindu festival that spans nine nights and is celebrated every year during autumn. Goddess Ambe Ma is worshipped and raas-garba is performed around her.

NGO: Non-Government Organisation.

NIIT: National Institute of Information Technology, an institute offering computer diploma courses.

O

Odisha: An eastern Indian state on the Bay of Bengal, earlier known as Orissa.

Odissi: A major Indian classical dance that originated in the Hindu temples of Odisha.

P

Pranayama: Yogic practice of focusing on one's breath.

Pucca Gujju: An absolute Gujarati, in every sense.

Puja: Prayer.

Purdah: Veil.

Pratul: Husband of Manjula Pooja Shroff, Founder and CEO of e-Infochips.

Prerna School for Dyslexics: A school founded by Manjula Pooja Shroff for children with special learning needs.

R

Raga: It is a unique and central feature of the classical Indian music tradition. It is a collection of pitches like a scale or mode in Western music.

Raja Hrudaya Chandra Deo: Younger brother of Manjula Pooja Shroff.

Raja Keerti Chandra Deo: Father of Manjula Pooja Shroff, also the ruler of Surangi Palace in Ichapuram.

Ramadevi Women's College: A college in Bhubaneswar, the capital city of Odisha.

Rani Mahal: A wing of Surangi Palace in Ichapuram, Odisha.

Rani Soubhagya Manjari Devi: Mother of Manjula Pooja Shroff.

Rani Srimati Devi: Grandaunt of Manjula Pooja Shroff.

Ray Kurzweil: An American inventor and futurist, Raymond Kurzweil is involved in fields like optical character recognition, text-to-speech synthesis, speech recognition technology and electronic keyboard instruments.

Reiki: A healing technique based on the principle that the therapist can channel energy into the patient by means of touch.

S

Secret Seven: A fictional group of child detectives created by children's writer Enid Blyton.

Shroffism: Manjula Pooja Shroff's philosophy of learning accumulated through experiences, people, situations and new platforms shared especially via social media.

Skill India: Skill India or the National Skills Development Mission of India is a campaign launched by Government of India. It is managed by the National Skills Development Corporation of India.

Srimati Laxman Manjari: Grandmother of Manjula Pooja Shroff.

St Joseph's Convent: A school in Cuttack, Odisha, where Manjula Pooja Shroff studied.

Surangi: Surangi Palace, located at the entrance of Ichapuram town in Odisha.

T

Teacher Eligibility Test: The minimum qualification required in India for a person to be eligible for an appointment as a teacher for classes I to VIII. The test is mandatory for teaching jobs in Indian government schools.

Thomas Hardy: An English novelist and poet.

U

USA: United States of America.

Utkal University: A public university in Bhubaneswar city in Odisha.

V

Visamo Kids: A Foundation and NGO that provides free education for kids in the state of Gujarat.

Vata-Pitta-Kapha: These are combinations and permutations of the primary functional energies in the body, comprising space, air, fire, water and earth, according to Ayurveda.

W

WhatsApp: A cross-platform centralised instant messaging mobile application.

Y

Yogasanas: It originally referred to a sitting meditation pose, but has now extended to refer to multiple postures that are performed to benefit the body and mind.

3D: Three-dimensional computer graphics that provide the perception of depth. In the third stage of 3D modelling, the transformed images are rendered into objects with fine detail.

Some part of definitions and explanations have been taken from the internet for clarity and quick understanding.